KIDS EXPLORE AMERICA'S AFRICAN-AMERICAN HERITAGE

Westridge Young Writers Workshop

John Muir Publications
Santa Fe, New Mexico

Read this book and you will learn.
We, as all people, make the world turn.
Each person is different in his own special way.
We want you to know that that's okay.
You can learn from these people as you will see.
This book is for you—given from me!

This book is dedicated to people of different cultures, with the hope
that they are proud of who they are.

John Muir Publications, P.O. Box 613, Santa Fe, NM 87504
©1993 by Jefferson County School District No. R-1
Cover © 1993 by John Muir Publications
All rights reserved. Published 1992
Printed in the United States of America

First edition. Second printing February 1993

Library of Congress Cataloging-in-Publication Data
Kids explore America's African-American heritage / Westridge Young
    Writers Workshop. — 1st ed.
        p. cm.
    Summary: Examines the contributions of African-Americans to
American culture in such areas as music, food, literature, and
celebrations. Includes profiles of significant individuals.
    ISBN 1-56261-090-2
    1. Afro-Americans—Juvenile literature. [1. Afro-Americans.
2. Children's writings.] I. Westridge Young Writers Workshop.
E185.K46   1993
973' .0496073—dc20   92-32275
                                                          CIP
                                                          AC

Design Susan Surprise/ Ken Wilson
Typefaces Garamond and Helvetica
Typography Ken Wilson, John Muir Publications
Printer Banta Company

Distributed to the book trade by   Distributed to the education market by
W.W. Norton & Co., Inc.   The Wright Group
500 Fifth Avenue   19201 120th Avenue NE
New York, NY 10110   Bothell, WA 98011

Photo credits   Photo on page 16 courtesy of the Denver Public Library; photos on pages 5, 8, 11, 13,
                     17, 19, 20, 21, 28, 31, 34, 35, 36, 37, 38, and 71 courtesy of the Schomberg Collection
                     of the New York Public Library; photo on page 21 by Philippe Halsman.

CONTENTS

ACKNOWLEDGMENTS

We, the eighty-six student authors, are especially appreciative of the people of African-American heritage who shared their time and talent with us. We would also like to thank the Westridge Elementary School staff, the Westridge PTA, Ron Horn, and all of our teachers and volunteers for their confidence in us young writers.

Special thanks also go to several businesses and organizations for their financial support. Student scholarships were donated by King Soopers, Denver, Colorado, and Lakewood Civitan Club, Lakewood, Colorado. First Bank of Lakewood, Colorado, has given financial support to our program.

Many other people helped to make this book a reality. They are acknowledged in the list of other participants at the back of the book.

STUDENTS' PREFACE

As you read these pages, line by line,
Love and fun you're sure to find.
Whate'er your color it doesn't matter,
Look at the soul, not the sound of the chatter.
So listen to the words we tell,
They're loud and clear—just like a bell.
People are different, that's no lie.
Everyone's special like you and I.
Color, shape, size—they're no big deal,
It's what's inside you that is real.
Black or white, it's all the same,
So let's put an end to this silly game.
As you turn the pages of this book,
Turn around and take another look.
A perfect world the earth would be,
A land of peace and harmony,
If people would just treat each other
As if we were a sister or brother.

Beware! If you read this book, you will learn about parts of African-American heritage that you may not already know!

This book is written from a kid's point of view. It is fun to read. We authors are in grades 3 through 8, and we worked very hard to share with you some of the information we learned. We are excited because this book will help teach all people about the pride in African-American heritage.

Kids Explore America's African-American Heritage is not just for kids. Grown-ups should read it and learn from it, too. We hope it will help make our world a more peaceful and equal place to live.

TEACHERS' PREFACE

We accept the challenge of building a brighter future. We will not ignore the problems caused by racism in America. We pledge to continue to work for respect for all Americans.

The Kids Explore series is meant to be informative as well as to instill a sense of pride in the diverse heritages of America. The Westridge Young Writers Workshop is located at Westridge Elementary School in Jefferson County, a western suburb of Denver, Colorado. John Muir Publications of Sante Fe, New Mexico, was enthusiastic and brought its publishing expertise to our program. Together we are working to increase children's respect and understanding of America's many cultures.

Kids Explore America's African-American Heritage was written by eighty-six students in grades 3 through 8. We, twenty-seven teachers and fourteen high school mentors, directed and assisted in writing and illustrating our exploration of African-American culture. Students experienced many aspects of African-American heritage, including history, heroes, celebrations, food, art, music, dance, folktales, language, and "real people" (African-Americans from across our country today). They explored these aspects of the culture, researched information, worked on word processing, organized, wrote, proofread, and illustrated. After nine wonderful, hectic days, we celebrated all we had learned together.

While our young authors enhanced their writing skills and enriched their knowledge of African-American heritage, we earned graduate college credit through a course entitled "Integrating African-American Studies into the School Curriculum."

Most of us were African-American teachers, mentors, and students who now live throughout the Denver metropolitan area. We have previously lived in many different parts of our country and shared our diverse knowledge of our culture. We were an enthusiastic group who explored ways to integrate African-American culture into the curriculum, enriched our knowledge of publishing procedures, and enhanced our skills in teaching all aspects of the writing process.

Although we all share a deep respect for the African-American heritage, the most important thing we share is a wish to increase the awareness of the many diverse cultures that make up our country. We are risk takers, innovators, and believers in a brighter tomorrow. We sincerely believe that if concerned individuals ignore the racism that is growing in our society, America will have even greater problems in the future. We have accepted the challenge to implement change in America's schools. We have written a resource to be used in America's homes and classrooms to teach respect and understanding of different heritages in our country.

Remember to ask your bookstores, libraries, and schools about our book. Look for *Kids Explore America's Hispanic Heritage*, and watch for future titles in the Kids Explore series.

HISTORY

The history of blacks
Is often out of whack
But our book has put it back.

We have struggled through time
And we hope you keep in mind
That we are important to all of
  mankind.

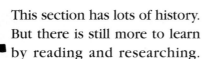

This section has lots of history. But there is still more to learn by reading and researching. We tell about some of the important events that brought African-Americans to where they are today.

As you read this chapter, try to remember that sometime in your heritage, no matter what your race is, one of your ancestors may have been a slave. All races have been victims of slavery. For example, at one time, the Romans conquered the Greeks. When the Greek people were defeated, they became slaves to the Romans. If they didn't cooperate, they were killed. Lots of people celebrate Saint Patrick's Day, but they may not know that St. Patrick was a slave

to Irish tribes in Ireland. It is important to realize that African-Americans are not the only people who have been slaves.

In this chapter, you will read that Africans had a rich heritage before they came to America. You will see that in America, which has a government based on a constitution that says everyone is created equal, African-Americans did not have freedom and were not treated as equals. You will read how the slaves started to gain their freedom through the underground railroad and the Civil War.

You will also read about the civil rights movement and the people who worked hard to make everyone equal through nonviolent protests like talking, petitions, sit-ins, and the March on Washington.

We hope you will learn not to judge people by their color but by their character. And we hope you will learn something new about African-American history.

BEFORE AMERICA

The ancestors of African-Americans made many contributions to other cultures of the world for which they have never been given fair credit. A lot of things found in Greek, European, and Asian cultures actually started in Africa. In fact, some scholars believe that mankind began in Africa. This is based on the fact that man-made tools over two million years old were found in East Africa. People thought the Lucy skeleton found in Europe was the oldest evidence of mankind until much older bones were discovered in Kenya, Africa. These bones are believed to be four million years old.

The land of Africa was and still is a rich land, not only because of the many resources (silver, gold, and diamonds) but also because the land is made up of such a variety of landscapes. There are great deserts in the north, lush rain forests in the center, and great rolling plains in the south and along the coasts. History books tell us the most important resource was the people, who built great nations and kingdoms long before most of the world became great.

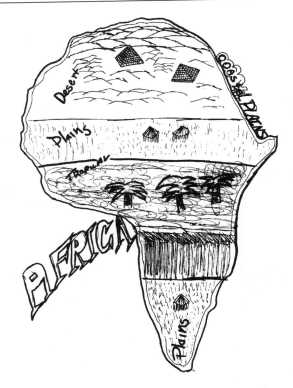

Egypt, on the northern coast of Africa, at one time was not much more than a group of city-states. These were cities that had separate governments and worked independently. These city-states were made into the Empire of Egypt around 3100 B.C. This was the first great nation in Africa and one of the greatest in world history. It reached its height at about 1400 B.C. and produced many great rulers. One of these, Thutmoses III, ruled from about 1500 to 1450 B.C. This great black leader controlled a kingdom 2,000 miles long and was known for his military power. The kingdom of Kush, another nation located just south of the Egyptian empire, was founded about 1,000 years after Egypt united. It lasted from 2000 B.C. to A.D. 350. Kush,

which conquered Egypt in about 700 B.C., was the first African nation to specialize in iron mining and manufacturing. Toward the end of the kingdom of Kush, around A.D. 300, a great empire, named Ghana, was getting started in the western part of Africa. This kingdom, the first major nation of West Africa, lasted about 1,000 years (A.D. 300 to 1200) and was known for its wealth and trade. This nation was conquered by the Mandingo (Mandinka), a group of people it once ruled. The Mandingo people formed a nation called Mali, which means "where the Mansa (master or king) resides." The Mali kingdom lasted only two hundred years but stretched 1,500 miles eastward from the Atlantic Ocean. One of its great black leaders, Mansa Musa, who ruled from A.D. 1312 to 1337, established the Great University of Sankore in the city of Timbuktu. This university was one of the largest in the world. During this time, a group of West Africans known as Moors invaded, con-

quered, and ruled Spain for 700 years (A.D. 711 to 1400). The Moors, who were great shipbuilders and sailors, taught the Spanish people the skills of making maps and round globes, paving, and lighting streets.

We do know that there were many more great nations and rulers (kings and queens) in Africa who also contributed much to civilization as we know it. We just wanted to tell you about a few great nations that existed long before Europe was developed.

Here are a few more examples of discoveries made by early Africans. An Egyptian contribution was the introduction of papyrus (paper). Another was the beginning of a belief in one god. The pharaoh (an Egyptian king), Akhenaton, taught his people to believe in one god. Another wonderful contribution of the black people was the first university. In the beginning, it was called Grand Lodge

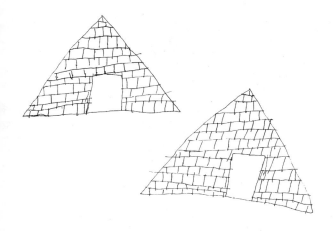

of Wa'at. This name was later changed by the Greeks, who called it Luxor. Imhotep, an African man who lived about 2800 B.C., was the father of medicine. Many sources state that the first doctor was Hippocrates, but Hippocrates was born 2,000 years after Imhotep. Many historians tell us that astronomy, map making, and the solar calendar started in Africa. Africans also discovered the basics of geometry, such as angles, circumference, and radius. Geometry was used in the building of the pyramids as early as 2664 B.C., just as it has been used in constructing modern buildings such as the Eiffel Tower and the Washington Monument. The concept of government and kings and queens originated in Africa as well.

We hope this information will help you understand why African-Americans have such pride in their heritage. There are many books you could read to find out more about Africa.

THE BEGINNING OF SLAVERY IN AMERICA

Originally, not all Africans in the colonies were slaves. Some were indentured servants. An indentured servant was a person who had to work for another person for no pay until his debt was paid in labor, usually a period of from two to seven years. After indentured servants had completed their time, they would be given food, clothes, seeds, tools, and a little money to start their own life in America. White indentured servants sometimes escaped. Their skin was fair, so if they managed to escape, they could mix in with other whites and were hard to capture. White settlers also tried to make Native Americans (Indians) their servants. They found out that the Indians didn't make good slaves. They would escape and go back to their tribes, or they would kill themselves. White settlers started to bring in Africans to be their indentured servants

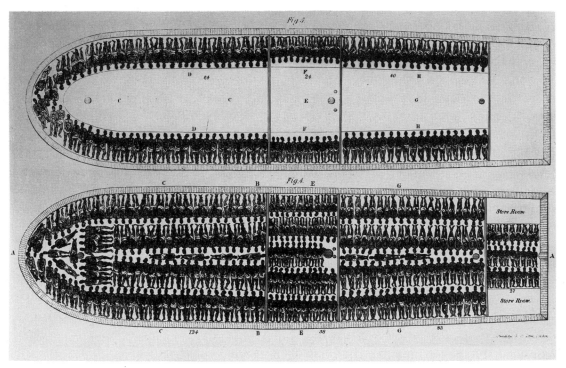

Slave traders crowded as many slaves as possible onto ships to increase their profit.

and do their work for them. Unfortunately, people from Africa didn't stay indentured servants. Something far worse happened. They became slaves.

Close your eyes and imagine you are sound asleep in your home. All of a sudden, a bunch of men burst into your room and kidnap you. You are placed in chains and sent on a long journey to America as a lifetime servant for a white settler. This actually happened to many men, women, and children who became slaves in the American colonies. Conditions on the slave ships were horrible. Since money was so important, slave traders almost always tried to bring as many people to the Americas as possible. Africans were packed in the cargo

holds of ships. Many slaves even died at sea.

After slaves got off the ship from Africa, they were rounded up like cattle and taken to market for auction. Even if they came with their family, they would probably be split up. Life never got any better.

Many slaves were bought to work on plantations. A plantation is a big farm that raises corn, tobacco, beans, cotton, and cattle. When Eli Whitney invented the cotton gin in 1798, cotton was suddenly a big moneymaker. The cotton gin separated seeds by cranking the cotton through a small set of comblike teeth. Anyone with slaves and land would plant as much as possible to get a piece of the action. Slave labor was in even greater demand than before. Slaves might have to pick from dawn to dusk, and the shells of the cotton blistered their fingers. Plantation owners needing more workers bought more and more slaves as their work load increased. The slaves planted, harvested, cared for crops, did laundry, and cooked. Meanwhile, the owners were free to do other things and make money from the sweat of their slaves.

Life was hard for the black slaves on the plantations. They had to work by hand in the hot sun, from sunup to sundown. The slaves had to stay on the plantation, and it became their world. They lost all the things they had known—like their culture, their language, their families, and their freedom. Even the weather and the climate were different.

Slaves quite often were treated badly. We heard of one slave owner who whipped his slave to death because he called him mister instead of master. Another slave was whipped because he looked at the dead slave and started to cry. If slaves were caught trying to escape, they were severely punished by whipping, jail, or death. Most slave owners, or masters as they were called, didn't want to punish their slaves with death because the slaves were considered valuable property. When slaves were lucky enough to escape, they had little chance of freedom because of their skin color.

Although many slaves were treated poorly, they brought with them and added wonderful things to America. The slaves knew how to plant and when to harvest crops because they did this according to a solar calendar in Africa. Blacks were creative and talented. They were good woodcarvers, basket makers, weavers, potters, iron workers, and chemists.

The "underground railroad" helped many black slaves to freedom. This meant going where slavery was illegal, to the free states, northern or western territories, or Canada. The so-called railroad started near the middle of the 1800s. In 1830, a man named Tice Davids escaped from his Kentucky owner. Tice swam across a river in sight of his owner and disappeared on the other side. The owner said he must have taken an underground road. Slaves heard about Tice Davids and started to use this escape route, which later was called the underground railroad. It was called "underground" because it was hidden and "railroad" because it was used often. It was not a real railroad. It had secret passageways, and the slaves used all kinds of transportation to get to a free place to live. Sometimes they walked, rode in a horse-drawn carriage, or took a boat.

The underground railroad needed many people to make it run safely. People who felt that slavery was wrong hid runaway slaves in their homes and farms, even though it could get them in trouble. People had passages in their houses with walls that would move so that slaves could hide behind them. Many people who were against slavery used their homes as stops on the underground railroad. These houses were called "stations." "Stationmasters" were the owners of the houses and other hiding places. The slaves were called "passengers" or "merchandise." One slave named Hezekiah Hill hid for one year under the floor of his friend's house before his friend could get a boat and take him to freedom. A slave named Henry Hill used an unusual way to escape. He put himself in a box and mailed himself north to freedom, earning the nickname "Box" Brown.

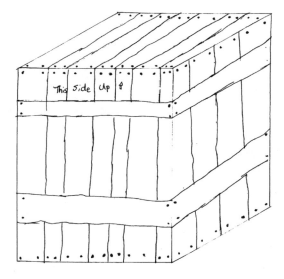

EMANCIPATION

The underground railroad finally stopped running in 1865 at the end of the Civil War. The Civil War brought an end to slavery and put America on the road to racial equality. The people who worked the underground railroad, though, weren't the only ones who didn't agree with slavery. Another group of people, called Abolitionists, were active in their cities. They drew up petitions against slavery and gave them to their leaders in Congress. Some worked hard to help free black people in their towns and cities.

Harriet Tubman, Frederick Douglass, and Sojourner Truth were outstanding African-American leaders of the Abolitionists in the 1800s. They were brave because they spoke up for African-American rights during a time in America when blacks had few rights and little freedom.

During the Civil War, the South fought to keep slavery. Plantation owners really needed many people to work for little or nothing to make money. The northern states had a different economy and didn't need slaves. They built factories, using machines and developing natural resources. The North wanted to put an end to slavery because they could hire blacks to work in their factories as cheap labor.

Do you know who the Great Emancipator was? He was President Abraham Lincoln, and he delivered the speech known as the Emancipation Proclamation in 1862. "To emancipate" means to set free from an influence or authority. A "proclamation" is an official public announcement. The Emancipation Proclamation was an important part of the

President Abraham Lincoln delivered the Emancipation Proclamation in 1862.

Civil War because it helped end slavery in the United States.

The Civil War was still being fought when Lincoln issued the Emancipation Proclamation. Many things did not change for the northern, or Union, side because they were already free. In fact, it freed no one right away, but it had a great effect. Runaway slaves moved to northern states and to Canada. Though it made the South mad, it made the North look good in Europe because people there didn't believe in slavery either. Although the Emancipation Proclamation did not officially end slavery in America, on December 18, 1865, the 13th amendment to the Constitution did. It said,

The Emancipation Proclamation of 1862 was the official public announcement that led to the end of slavery in the United States.

"Neither slavery nor involuntary servitude, except as a punishment for crime whereof the party shall have been duly convicted, shall exist within the U.S."

By the end of the Civil War, about 180,000 blacks were fighting in Lincoln's Union army and about 30,000 in the Union navy. Thirty-eight thousand blacks died fighting for the Union cause. Lincoln rewarded the black effort by announcing their freedom.

RECONSTRUCTION

After the Civil War, the South was in terrible condition because that's where many of the battles had been fought. The North was in excellent shape because it had factories, farms, and railroads, all of which developed even more from the war effort.

Reconstruction was the time in United States history that followed the Civil War. It was when the North and South finally made peace with each other. It was a time to reconstruct or rebuild from the damage done to the South during the war and a time to heal the hard feelings in the country. This period in history (1865-1877) gave African-Americans some of the freedom and rights they deserved. However, during this period, many African-Americans had freedom but little else. They had no land, no money, no means to live. Some worked on the same land that they had worked on as slaves, but now they worked as sharecroppers. Sharecroppers would grow crops and share the profits with the landowners. Many blacks were forced to move north to the cities as they looked for work and a better life. Unfortunately, many ended up living in poverty in the new ghettos with other immigrant groups and ethnic minorities. They often lived in poor housing, had low-paying jobs, and paid high prices for food and clothing.

Reconstruction solved some problems. The North and the South decided to join together again as the United States of America and work to build one strong nation. Congress passed laws to protect African-Americans and gave them the right to vote. But other problems still remained. Most southern whites still did not accept African-Americans as equals. Living and working conditions hadn't improved much for African-Americans. Pretty soon, the North forgot about Reconstruction, and southern whites ignored many of the rights the African-Americans had won earlier. To the whites, slavery was necessary for their way of life. Blacks were kept from voting by the use of violence, poll taxes, and other discriminatory practices. The Ku Klux Klan (KKK) was organized, and its members beat and murdered blacks and their white supporters. Reconstruction really didn't solve the problems of prejudice in America.

THE ROAD TO FREEDOM

Another important period of time in U.S. history centers around the civil rights movement. Civil rights are important because they give all people many kinds of freedoms and enable them to participate in society equally. Going places that you choose, sitting where you want, saying what you believe, and going to any school you choose are all examples of civil rights. This makes all people more respectful of other races and cultures. The following events in U.S. history encouraged people to get along better.

In 1905, in Niagara Falls, New York, W. E. B. Du Bois called a meeting so that African-Americans could talk about how to deal with their unequal treatment. It was called the Niagara Movement. It was a gathering of black scholars who felt that first-class citizenship should be guaranteed to all blacks. Not everyone who came agreed with Du Bois, but the group did make a list of changes that needed to be made. The movement only lasted four years due to lack of money within the all-black membership.

William E. B. Du Bois, scholar, writer, and leader for black rights in the early 1900s

In 1910, Du Bois again tried to organize the African-Americans. He started the NAACP with some of the people from the Niagara Movement and with sympathetic whites. NAACP stands for National Association for the Advancement of Colored People. This group became the number one organization with the knowledge and the money to fight for justice for black Americans in the government. The NAACP was very active during the years that Martin Luther King, Jr., was working for racial equality. The NAACP still provides legal help for black people with problems that affect their community or that affect them as individuals. They raise money through donations from kind and concerned people.

In 1911, the National Urban League was founded by Booker T. Washington in New York City. He disagreed with Du Bois about how to help blacks. Du Bois thought heritage was most important, and Washington thought jobs were most important. The National Urban League still helps African-Americans find jobs and housing and gives them emotional support in big cities.

Another time black people were noticed was during the Harlem Renaissance, which began in 1912 in Harlem, a section of New York City. This was an important time in black culture, because America at large began to show a growing appreciation for the work of black artists. During this time, black artists in art, music, dance, and literature really started doing their stuff. They knew this

was their chance for white people to learn more about black culture. However, though blacks were being recognized for their artistic accomplishments, they still faced discrimination and problems at work.

In 1919, Samuel Gompers started the American Federation of Labor because he said he wanted to end discrimination of all people in the workplace. Since Gompers couldn't end discrimination all by himself, other people helped. A. Philip Randolph had the goal of getting better working conditions for the many black people who worked for the Pullman Company. They wanted more money, a shorter workweek, and equal treatment. Randolph tripled the number of black people working for the Pullman Company. He told people to go in and tell their bosses to give them what they wanted. Black employees said they wouldn't work if they didn't get better working conditions. The workers wanted to prove that the company needed them a lot by showing what it would be like if no one did their jobs. This plan eventually worked. They received a contract that improved their working conditions and also doubled, then tripled, their weekly pay.

In 1929, the Great Depression began. It lasted through the 1930s. During this time, many people of all races were without jobs, money, and food. President Franklin D. Roosevelt wanted to relieve the hunger and poverty of all people, and he was also opposed to racial discrimination.

Mary McLeod Bethune, a black woman, was named the head of the National Youth Organization of Concern by President Roosevelt. This organization gave money to college students to continue their education. Mary Bethune was also very active in civil rights issues. She founded the National Council of Negro Women, a group that helped black people with social, economic, and political concerns. Mrs. Bethune and Mrs. Roose-

Military units were segregated through World War II.

velt were very good friends. Mrs. Bethune was the first black woman to have an official job advising the president.

After the depression, people were still angry that African-Americans didn't have equal rights. Have you ever been so angry at something that you wanted to walk to the White House, where the president lives, and let him know how mad you were? Blacks and whites in 1941 decided they were fed up with discrimination. Thousands of people threatened to march on Washington to end discrimination in the defense industry, which was building weapons, ships, and

planes for the military. Black leaders like A. Philip Randolph and Bayard Rustin planned the march. Fortunately, the rally never took place because President Roosevelt jumped in and assured people that he would end discrimination in the government.

How did over a million African-Americans feel fighting during World War II, when the armed forces were still segregated? Black servicemen hated it, and so did those blacks who weren't in the military. Most blacks in the air force were maintenance workers because they were not allowed to become pilots until a black training center was opened in

Tuskegee, Alabama, in 1942. In the navy, most blacks were cooks until 1945, when they were allowed to become officers. In the army, as well as other services, blacks were kept together as whole units. Some black units such as the 99th Pursuit Air Force Squadron and the 761st Army Tank Battalion fought heroically. In 1948, after the war ended, William Hastie, A. Philip Randolph, and Thurgood Marshall worked toward having the armed forces desegregated. They told the black men not to enlist in the military if everything was still segregated. Harry Truman, who was president at the time, knew he needed black men in the military, so he issued an order that guaranteed equal treatment and equal opportunity for African-Americans in the armed forces.

A very important event in the civil rights movement took place in 1954, when the case of *Brown v. Board of Education of Topeka, Kansas,* went to court. This was a case arguing that black and white kids should be treated the same by being allowed to go to the same schools. Black children didn't like going to separate schools because many white schools had more books and better teachers and facilities. Often, blacks had to travel farther to go to all-black schools. For two years, *Brown v. Board of Education* was heard in several courts. The last was the U.S. Supreme Court, and their decision was to desegregate all public schools. Even though this often meant going where they weren't wanted, black people were pleased.

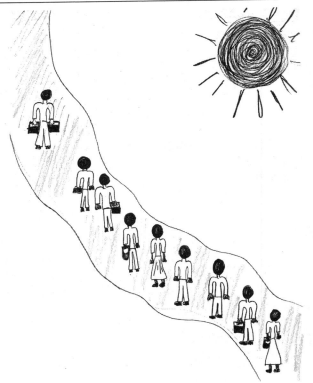

One of the most important persons in the civil rights movement was Reverend Dr. Martin Luther King, Jr. Dr. King's followers used nonviolent ways to get their ideas across.

On December 1, 1955, someone decided to take a stand against the white belief that black people were not as good as white people. Many racial practices in America at that time were known as "Jim Crow laws." They might seem silly now, but they were really happening then. Throughout the South, blacks had to use different bathrooms, schools, and drinking fountains. Signs read "White Only" and "Colored Only," and many businesses refused to serve blacks. Blacks had to sit in the back of the buses and in different sections of restaurants. They received their wages

Reverend Dr. Martin Luther King, Jr., civil rights leader whose philosophy of nonviolence inspired generations of Americans

from different pay windows. There was even a rule that black and white cotton mill workers couldn't look out the same window. Some unfair racial practices were just as common in the northern states—but without posted signs.

Then there was a major event one cold December day in Montgomery, Alabama. A tired woman took a stand. This was Rosa Parks. You see, if the white section of a bus became full, then the black people on the bus had to give up their seats. But on this day, Ms. Parks was too tired to stand. She refused to give up her seat. She was arrested. This one event led to the Montgomery Bus Boycott.

The Montgomery Bus Boycott was led by E. D. Nixon. He passed out leaflets that urged all of the blacks not to ride on the buses. The boycott was even announced in Sunday church services and newspapers. This was a hard thing for some people to do because the bus was their only way to get to work. Many people couldn't afford to miss work and lose a day's pay. Some people ended up carpooling or riding mules. Some even walked many miles to work.

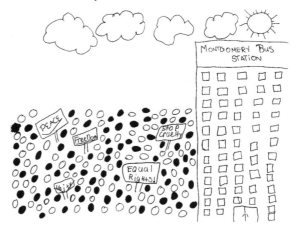

Normally the buses were crowded, but on the first day of the boycott there were hardly any blacks on the bus. The plan worked so well that Nixon called a community meeting at a local church. So many people came that they had to sit outside on the lawn and listen through speakers. Nixon suggested that they boycott all buses until they were desegregated. Then Reverend Dr. Martin Luther King, Jr., stood up and gave a speech telling the people that it was time to stop letting other people keep them from being free. His speech was so powerful that the crowd went from quiet and calm to a standing ovation.

Martin Luther King, Jr., is, without a doubt, the most famous and respected civil rights leader in America. He did many things to help all people become sensitive about other cultures and races. Many civil rights organizations, such as CORE and SNCC, have used his model of nonviolence in an effort to try to achieve a better way of life. Dr. King believed strongly in the power of peaceful protests (like organized boycotts and sit-ins) instead of violence. Even today, many groups use his ways of peaceful protest to make positive social and political changes.

Lots of publicity surrounded the Montgomery boycott, and southern blacks decided to take an even bigger stand. They started holding protests like sit-ins and rallies to show that they wouldn't live with segregation, or Jim Crow laws, any longer. Protest songs like "We Shall Overcome" and "Blowing in the Wind," as well as many gospel songs, became themes of the growing movement.

Later on in the movement, freedom riders, people sworn to nonviolence, took "freedom rides" to test bus, air, and rail lines for desegregation. Everywhere the freedom riders went they were met with violence. Huge mobs of racists beat people, burned buses, and terrorized the black and white freedom riders. Sometimes, police and National Guard troops didn't do anything to stop the violence that was going on right in front of them. Many ambulance drivers and hospitals in the area didn't do anything to help the injured, bleeding protestors. In fact, many protestors were permanently disabled or killed during the riots. The

Boycotts and sit-ins were powerful peaceful protests.

problem got so bad that even the president, John F. Kennedy, and his brother, Robert Kennedy, who was attorney general of the United States, had to step in to try to stop the violence. They ordered the governors of Alabama and Mississippi to cooperate with the freedom riders, but the governors still didn't listen. They allowed the police to beat and arrest the freedom riders. President Kennedy recommended that blacks vote in great numbers so that the prejudiced sheriffs and judges, who allowed segregation, could be voted out of office. This worked, and the buses were eventually desegregated. The freedom riders went on to do other things.

The year 1963 was a hard one for Martin Luther King, Jr., and his followers. All over the country there were strong racist feelings. In Alabama, George Wallace was elected governor

because he said that there would be no integration in Alabama, ever. As a result, public places like swimming pools, parks, playgrounds, and golf courses were closed just to keep blacks out. This made Dr. King sad, so he decided to make Birmingham, Alabama, the next target of his protests against segregation. Fifteen thousand of Dr. King's supporters were arrested for protesting even though they were peaceful. Even some six-year-olds were arrested.

By the summer of 1963, blacks were demanding full equality. Many black organizations chose August 28 for a march on Washington, D.C. The leaders of the march expected only a few thousand people to attend. Instead, over 310,000 people came. Two thousand freedom buses and thirty freedom trains brought black people to Washington, D.C., from all over the country. Hour after hour, people arrived at the Lincoln Memorial. In fact, the entire area between the Washington Monument and the Lincoln Memorial became a sea of people, black and white, fighting prejudice together. At the time, it was the largest demonstration ever held in the United States. It was at this time that Martin Luther King Jr., gave his famous "I Have a Dream" speech.

Martin Luther King, Jr., wasn't the only civil rights leader. The Black Power Movement also fought for civil rights, but it wasn't as peaceful as Dr. King's forces. They didn't want to wait for things to happen. They wanted to force changes immediately.

In the summer of 1963, over 300,000 people attended the March on Washington for People's Rights.

Malcolm X, an important spokesman for equal rights

One of the people involved in the Black Power Movement was Malcolm X. Malcolm changed his last name from Little to X because the name Little was given to his family by slave masters. The X represents his unknown black ancestry. When he was a child, he fell into a life of crime and quit school. He was arrested when he was a teenager. While he was in jail, he read a lot about freedom and started to work toward freedom for blacks. There he became a follower of Elijah Muhammad, the leader of the Black Muslim church. When he got out of jail, he worked with Muhammad as an assistant minister. Muhammad's health was poor so he appointed Malcolm the national minister. Other Muslims became jealous of this. Malcolm began to suspect his enemies were turning Muhammad against him. Malcolm and other mem-

bers of the Black Muslims began to disagree about how to handle certain situations. Even Muhammad began to feel that Malcolm was a threat to his leadership. In 1964, Malcolm announced he was leaving the group. He started a new group, the Organization for Afro-American Unity. This was a protest group. Malcolm was known for his strong ideas and for being outspoken. In 1965, he was assassinated, but even today, his memory is still present in the fight for equality.

Another group that was part of the Black Power Movement was the Black Panthers. This group opened schools to educate people about black heritage. They organized food distribution centers for the poor. They also educated people about their rights as citizens. The Black Panthers were people who didn't mind doing violent things to gain civil rights. One of the things they would do was to follow police cars and see if they were going to stop black people and pick on them. In their cars they carried guns and books that explained state laws. If the police were mean, the Black Panthers would get out of their cars and get involved. The police didn't like them getting involved. They wanted to get a law passed so the Black Panthers couldn't carry guns. The day that the government was going to decide about the issue, some Black Panthers went to the meeting and spoke about their beliefs and rights. They caused no violence. Although the Black Panthers told the court that they did nothing wrong, they were arrested and sent to jail for six months.

Angela Davis, educator, Black Power Movement leader for the Black Panther Party (Photo by Philippe Halsman)

Angela Davis was a member of the Black Panthers. She was in charge of political education. She went around talking about the rights black people should have. She was especially interested in the case of three black prisoners. These men had been accused of murdering a guard at Soledad Prison. She thought this was unfair because there was no proof that they were involved in the crime. Jonathan Jackson, the brother of George Jackson, one of the prisoners, kidnapped the judge, district attorney, and several jurors during the trial of the three men. He said that if they didn't free his brother, he would kill his hostages. When Jonathan Jackson and the hostages got to the van, a bunch of shots hit the van, and some of the people he kidnapped were found dead. The police never found out who fired the shots, but Angela Davis was arrested because she was the one accused of owning the guns used in the kidnapping. The charges were dismissed in July 1972.

These events and people are some of the important ones involved in the civil rights movement. We hope this information makes you want to read and learn more about these times, because we feel they are full of ideas, challenges, strengths, and hopes. The goals and hopes of these people were meant to create equality and brotherly love. We believe we need more of this.

AMERICA TODAY

Many things have aided in the progress of African-Americans. Peaceful protests, political reforms, education, and better jobs have all helped. The civil rights battle opened the doors of opportunity for many African-Americans but still left our country with racial problems. Education is the real key to changing people's attitudes and their positions in society. Overall, education has improved in the African-American community, although we are still working toward equality.

Many black students who are able to attend college often do so only after fighting hard to get loans and scholarships. During the 1980s, the government cut back on student loans, making it even harder for blacks to go to college.

Education is always a big concern across the country. Many citizens and or-

ganizations worry that schools aren't doing a good job, and many kids of all cultures are dropping out. Some African-Americans are able to go on to college by using the United Negro College Fund. This is a nonprofit, fund-raising association for 41 of the biggest black colleges in the United States. Its members include 39 private colleges and universities and 2 graduate schools. You have probably heard the saying, "A mind is a terrible thing to waste." This means that we have got to provide a chance for all people to get an education so that we have as many people working toward the growth of our country as possible. Education puts many more people into the scientific, medical, and business fields to create a better society for all of us.

Education is not the only challenge facing African-Americans today. There are still the problems of poverty, violence, and racism. Poverty can be found in any black neighborhood and in any city or town in this country. This is a very big problem because joblessness and the lack of opportunities can lead to violence.

Some people believe that violence comes from anger when people cannot control their own lives. Name calling and beatings are signs of a war between races that may never end. Leaders and their followers are trying to stop this war. Some have died while fighting, and some have lived to tell their story. For example, in 1991, in Los Angeles, a man named Rodney King was arrested for reckless driving and was beaten up by the police. Another man happened to videotape the whole thing. The police officers who beat Rodney King were

taken to court in 1992. The jury found them not guilty because the police said that Mr. King was resisting arrest. Many people in our nation were upset about this. It was a real scary time. There were disturbances and riots in several places across our country, but those in Los Angeles were the worst. Some people who were mad about the police beating Rodney King went out and beat up other people and burned down many businesses in the Los Angeles area. Other people broke into stores and stole things. Rodney King asked people to stop acting this way. He told them that we all have to learn to live together. Throughout the riot, all races were involved in the fighting. Afterward, people of all races were involved in cleaning up the devastation from the riots.

There are still many problems with racism in the United States. Thanks to some people, equal rights laws have been passed. Blacks have more opportunities for employment and advancement, and they have a better chance to get an education beyond the public high schools. More blacks are being accepted by universities. In politics, African-American people have run for public offices like president, governor, and mayor. For example, Shirley Chisholm was the first black *and* the first woman to run for president in the 1970s. Jesse Jackson ran for president in 1988. Wellington Webb was elected mayor of Denver, Colorado, in 1991. His opponent was also black. The first black woman astronaut to go on a space shuttle mission was Mae Jameson. Also, more blacks are getting jobs as managers, police officers, surgeons, lawyers, and FBI agents.

Some of the protests in the last twenty years have been successful in making a statement about fairness for all races. Others were not so successful in making a change but have made a mark for people to remember. At least people across our nation recognize we still have a big problem with racism and fairness. Many more people have started to look at these problems. Together we can do away with racism and prejudice.

We hope to see a future with fairness for African-Americans and people of all races. We hope to have more and better jobs for all people so they can take care of themselves and live a better life. We hope that this book will help to make people of all races understand that everyone is equal.

FAMOUS FIRSTS AND HEROES

The battles they have fought,
Have given us a lot.
Always working at their best,
They tried hard to pass the test.

African-Americans have suffered, worked, and grown throughout the history of America. They have used strength, determination, and wisdom to overcome problems. They have strengthened the United States by improving their own lives as well as the lives of other people in this country. For example, their long struggle for civil rights has resulted in laws to end discrimination against all races, religions, and cultures. These laws guarantee the right to vote and other rights to all U.S. citizens.

In this chapter, we will tell you about people who became famous by doing things first. We call these people famous firsts. We also tell about some outstanding heroes among the African-American people. They are civil rights leaders, inventors, scientists, doctors, educators, religious leaders, people in government, explorers, athletes, and others. We will tell you about African-Americans who are well known and some African-Americans whom most of us have never heard of. We have chosen seven people to write about in greater depth. We couldn't write long biographies on everyone, so we did this with only these few. The people we have written about are arranged in order by the year they were born. This helped us to see which people were alive at the same time and when they made their contributions. There are so many people to write about that it was difficult to choose. We have left out some of the most famous heroes because these people have many books written about them already, and you can read about them in other sections of our book. For example, you will find out something about George Washington Carver and Mary McLeod Bethune in the food section. We hope that you will go to the library and do research on more great African-Americans. If it weren't for people like these, the world would be a different place today.

FEATURED BIOGRAPHIES

Lucy Terry Prince (1730-1821)

Lucy Terry Prince was the first recognized African-American poet and a fighter for the rights of African-Americans.

Ms. Prince was captured in Africa, at the age of five, brought to this country, and sold to a couple in Deerfield, Massachusetts. She was sixteen when Indians attacked Deerfield. She was a nurse, caring for the injured. What happened affected her so much that she wrote a poem based on the Indian attack. Her poem was called "The Bar's Fight."

Later she met her husband-to-be, Abijah Prince. He had been a slave who fought in the militia during the French and Indian war. Mr. Prince was given his freedom and three very valuable pieces of land in Northfield, Massachusetts.

Mr. Prince bought Lucy's freedom from her owners, and in 1756 they were

married and moved to Guilford, Vermont, where he had been given a one-hundred-acre farm by his employer. Abijah and Lucy Terry Prince had six children. After a few years, one of their neighbors tried to claim the couple's farm. Lucy Terry Prince rode to the city and told the governor's council. The council heard Ms. Prince's complaint and ruled in her favor. Ms. Prince returned home feeling good, because never before in American history had an African-American woman been able to get the attention of such high officials and achieve that much success.

Lucy Prince's enthusiasm was dampened when she tried to enter her youngest son, Abijah, Jr., in the new Williams College. No matter what the Princes tried, the officials at Williams College wouldn't let him attend. Ms.

Prince and her family continued to go on in spite of this setback. In 1794, Mr. Prince died. He was buried on the Guilford farm. For eighteen years, Ms. Prince rode horseback over the mountains from Sunderland, where she had moved, to visit his grave.

Later, a white neighbor wanted some of the Prince property in Sunderland. Ms. Prince again fought to keep all her land by taking it to court. The Vermont Supreme Court heard Ms. Prince's argument, and again the ruling was in her favor.

Benjamin Banneker (1731-1806)

Benjamin Banneker was the first African-American astronomer, mathematician, and surveyor. He was also an inventor. Mr. Banneker was born on November 9, 1731, in Baltimore, Maryland. He came into this world like every African-American should have—free. His grandmother came from England, and she taught Benjamin to read, write, and count. He would count caterpillars, weeds, stars, and even tobacco seeds. When he was twelve years old, he went to a nearby Quaker school. Learning was very easy for Mr. Banneker, and he loved science and math.

When he was only twenty-one, he made the first clock that strikes every hour. It was made completely of wood, even the gears, which he carved with a knife. He learned how to make the clock from a watch that he borrowed, took apart, studied, and then put back together in perfect condition. Mr. Banneker's clock kept perfect time for almost 40 years.

After making the striking clock, Benjamin borrowed books on astronomy, the study of stars and planets. He studied and studied until he knew all there was to know about astronomy. He correctly predicted a solar eclipse in 1789. For ten years, he made all the calculations to predict the movements of the stars and tides and wrote a yearly almanac. An almanac is a book that tells facts and makes predictions about the stars, moon, planets, tides, and weather. This almanac was the first scientific book written by an African-American. Mr. Banneker continued to work and study, becoming an expert in surveying (looking at and measuring land for exact size and shape, for maps) as well as astronomy and mathematics.

In 1791, President George Washington asked Mr. Banneker to help plan the streets and buildings in Washington, D.C. He was the first African-American to be asked to do a job by a president of the United States. Mr. Banneker also wrote a plan for world peace, which was the model one hundred years later for the League of Nations' plan proposed by President Woodrow Wilson. He worked for world peace and freedom for all people.

Benjamin Banneker also spoke out strongly against slavery and in favor of free public education for all children, black and white. He wrote a letter about this to Thomas Jefferson, who was so impressed that he sent a copy of Mr. Banneker's almanac to the Royal Academy of Sciences in Paris. With all his accomplishments, Benjamin Banneker proved wrong those people who believed that African-Americans were not smart and could not learn.

Leroy B. (Satchel) Paige (1906?-1987)

For twenty years, Satchel Paige was not allowed into baseball's white major leagues, even though he was an outstanding pitcher in the black leagues. But, by 1948, things were beginning to change in baseball, and African-Americans were allowed in the major leagues. Even though Mr. Paige was old for a baseball player, he still had a great pitching arm. No one knew exactly how old he was because he would never tell what year he had been born. Some say he was over 60 when he was signed by the Cleveland Indians. He had six victories as a relief pitcher.

Satchel Paige was a very tall, thin

man with very long arms that sometimes seemed to hang all the way down to his knees. He sometimes used a "windmill" windup, spinning his arm all the way around four or five times before letting go of the ball. On really important pitches, he used a double windup, spinning his arm one way for a while and then stopping and spinning it the other until he finally let go of the pitch. This drove the baseball fans and the opposing players wild.

Mr. Paige was quite a philosopher, and newspaper reporters liked to interview him. When a reporter asked him, "Satch, when they call you in from the bull pen, why do you walk to the pitching mound so slowly?" Satchel replied, "When they calls me in to pitch, usually they's in some kind of trouble. Only a fool rushes into trouble." One of

Satchel's favorite sayings was, "Don't never look back over your shoulder. Something might be gaining on you."

In 1971, Satchel Paige was elected into baseball's Hall of Fame and finally got his true recognition as one of the greatest pitchers ever.

Thurgood Marshall (1908-)

Justice Marshall was the first African-American to be appointed to the U.S. Supreme Court, the highest court in the land. When he was very young, his father taught him that not only did he have permission to fight but he *had* to fight to protect himself. It was this early training that sometimes got Thurgood Marshall into trouble at school.

While he was in college, Mr. Marshall joined the debating team. He found that he was good at fighting with words. After thinking about it, he decided he would be a lawyer, because lawyers helped people by fighting with words.

The University of Maryland would not let him attend its law school because he was an African-American, so he went to law school at Howard University, a major African-American university in Washington, D.C.

When he first became an attorney, Justice Marshall worked on cases that involved getting equal rights for African-Americans. In 1936, he went to New York City to work for the NAACP (National Association for the Advancement of Colored People), to which both blacks and whites belonged. Two years later, he became the chief counsel for the NAACP and won many cases for African-American citizens. He fought for the laws that would give them the right to go to any college, attend the same public schools as white children, take any seat on a bus or train, register to vote, and sit down and eat at any lunch counter.

Justice Marshall was nicknamed "Mr. Civil Rights." In 1961, President John F. Kennedy appointed him a federal judge. This appointment was not well liked by some senators from the South. The Senate must approve any man named by the president as a federal judge. It took one year for the Senate to approve Justice Marshall. In 1965, President Lyndon B. Johnson appointed him solicitor general in the Department of Justice. A solicitor general is the chief lawyer for the government. In 1967, President Johnson named Justice Marshall to the Supreme Court, the highest court in the United States of America. If you're on the Supreme Court, you're on it for life or until you get ill, die, or choose to retire.

Thurgood Marshall retired from the Supreme Court. On July 4, 1992, he received an award for his outstanding service.

Jackie Robinson (1919-1972)

Crack went the bat on the ball. Off went Jackie, the smallest kid in the neighborhood. Wow! Could he play ball! Jackie Robinson, the first African-American major league baseball player, was a talented, determined, and disciplined man. Jackie Robinson was born in a farmhouse on January 31, 1919, in Cairo, Georgia. He and his family moved to California. In the new neighborhood, they were the only black family on their block. Sometimes white neighbors were mean to them, and someone even burned a cross on their front yard.

In school there were two baseball teams that played at recesses and during lunch. Both teams wanted Mr. Robinson. He was very poor and wanted to save his mother the expense of giving him lunch, so he chose to play on the team that offered to share their lunches.

Mr. Robinson was an average student and a great athlete. He was quick and very competitive. Other players and coaches tried to upset him, get him angry, and make him forget about the game by making racial remarks. Their remarks only made Mr. Robinson more determined to win.

One day the phone rang at Mr.

Robinson's home. The caller was Branch Rickey, the manager of the Brooklyn Dodgers. He invited Mr. Robinson to join the team. This was the first time a black baseball player had been invited to play in the majors. His first game was in 1947, and he hit a home run. Fans still yelled bad comments and threw things at him, but through it all, he kept his temper. He knew that being the first black player wouldn't be easy, but he had the strength not to fight. In this way, he kept the door open for other blacks to play ball.

Mr. Robinson retired from baseball in 1957, but he kept himself busy. He became an active leader in the civil rights movement, making speeches and marching to gain equal rights for blacks. Five years after his retirement, he was elected into the Baseball Hall of Fame. On October 24, 1972, he died of a heart attack.

Jackie Robinson is considered one of America's greatest athletes, but he is also remembered for his courage. Today millions of African-American children dream of one day playing major league baseball.

Daniel "Chappie" James (1920-1978)

General Daniel James was the first African-American four-star general. He was a well-respected leader, speaker, and war hero. He was born in Florida in 1920. In 1942, he married Dorothy Watkins, and they had three children.

General James went to school at the Tuskegee Institute where he majored

in physical education. He also went for civilian pilot training. This is training for people who aren't in the military. He entered the Army Air Corps Aviation Cadet Program. He made the military his career and spent thirty-two years working hard to become a four-star general.

General James worked in many areas of the United States as well as other places around the world. He lived in England, Thailand, and the Libyan Arab Republic. He was also in charge of many defense programs, programs that are set up to keep the United States safe.

General James spent time in the Korean War as a fighter pilot. During the Korean War, he flew with Robin Old. They flew 101 missions. The other pilots nicknamed them Blackman and Robin after Batman and Robin. He also fought in the Vietnam War where he was a wing vice commander, which means he was the second man in charge of a group of fighter planes.

General James won over twenty military awards. Some of these are the Distinguished Service Medal, Distinguished Flying Cross, Combat Readiness Medal, and United Nations Service Medal. These medals are for terrific work in different areas. It is impressive that he received military awards for both wartime activities and peacetime activities. He also won several community awards.

General James gave many speeches about the importance of respecting and loving America. He believed strongly in the "American Dream." Many people asked him to speak at their meetings. People from all over came to hear his speeches because they were so good.

General James retired from the U.S. Air Force in 1978 because his heart was not working well. Fifteen thousand people came to his retirement party. Sammy Davis, Jr., brought his band and gave a two-hour concert. General James even got up and sang with him. A month later, he died from a heart attack.

Shirley Chisholm (1926-   )

Shirley Chisholm was the first woman in the U.S. House of Representatives. She worked hard to get job training, higher education, and business counseling for black people. She strongly believed that this was the key to getting a better life for African-Americans.

Ms. Chisholm's mother was a seamstress. Her father worked in a burlap factory. At an early age, she went to live with family members in Barbados in the West Indies, while her parents tried to save money for her education. She returned to Brooklyn at eleven and went to grade school and high school there. She earned a college scholarship. She graduated from Brooklyn College and Columbia University, where she earned a master's degree in elementary education. She worked as a nursery school teacher, was in charge of a day care center, and gave help and advice to the New York Department of Social Services. She became active in politics because the people in her neighborhood were looking for an honest, caring candidate.

While she was a representative, Ms. Chisholm sponsored the SEEK program, which offered students from minority groups the chance to have college level classes even if they hadn't graduated from high school. She also introduced the idea of a day care program that received its money from public taxes like we do today for our public school system.

Ms. Chisholm believed in using the information she learned in college and in her jobs. While she was in office she worked only on projects she felt she knew about. One time she was asked to work on an agriculture project. She refused, saying, "Put me somewhere where I can use my talents and knowledge." She was taken off that project and placed on another that she knew more about.

In 1972, Representative Chisholm announced that she wanted to run for president of the United States. It was unheard of at that time for any woman to run for president. But no one laughed. She was treated with the same respect as the men running for this office. People respected her decision, and even if she didn't win, people still thought she was terrific.

Ms. Chisholm has since retired and is now living quietly and enjoying her family.

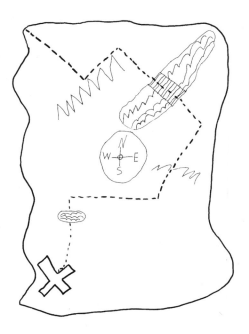

SHORT BIOGRAPHIES

Estevanico Dorantez (?-1539)

Estevanico Dorantez was a black Hispanic explorer. He lived in the 1500s. He sailed from Spain to the United States around the Florida Keys more than 400 years ago. The expedition he was on traveled for eight years through swamps and rivers to find Mexico City in 1536.

Mr. Dorantez's ship hit some coral reefs, and most of the crew died in the wreck. He and three of the crew were the only survivors. They walked for days. Then one day they found a large settlement of Indian pueblos. Mr. Dorantez opened the territory that is now New Mexico and Arizona. In 1539, the Indians killed Estevanico Dorantez. They were afraid that he was going to try to conquer them.

Elizabeth Freeman (1742-1829)

With the courage of a full army, Ms. Freeman worked to end slavery in Massachusetts. Elizabeth Freeman grew up in the middle of the 1700s during the colonial period. She lived in Massachusetts and worked as a slave for Colonel John Ashley. Ms. Freeman got sick of being a slave and felt that when the colonies won their independence, so should she.

After leaving the household of John Ashley and refusing to return, Ms. Freeman went looking for legal help to make sure she would stay free. She found a young lawyer named Theodore Sedgwick and asked him to help her gain freedom. She argued her case before Mr. Sedgwick and convinced him to take it.

In 1781, Ms. Freeman's case was heard by the county court in Great Barrington, Massachusetts. The court agreed that she was a free woman and that there would be no more slavery in Massachusetts. The judge made Colonel Ashley pay Ms. Freeman thirty shillings, a gold coin used in the British Commonwealth worth 100 cents in American money. After her victory, Ms. Freeman went to work for the Sedgwick family.

Olaudah Equiano (c.1745-c.1801)

Have you ever wanted to know what it would be like to be a slave? Well, Olaudah Equiano wrote a book explaining his life as a slave and how other slaves felt.

Mr. Equiano was born in 1745 in southern Nigeria, a part of Africa. When he was 11, he was playing in his front yard and three men came, picked him up, and carried him away. These men made him a slave.

Mr. Equiano had many slavemasters. Robert King, a merchant from Philadelphia, was the last person to buy him as a slave. Mr. King gave Mr. Equiano a new name, Gustavus Vassa, and taught him how to buy and sell the things in his store. This allowed Mr. Equiano to earn money to buy himself out of slavery. Mr. Equiano wrote a book, published in 1789, about his adventures as a slave. It was called *The Interesting Narrative of the Life of Olaudah Equiano, or Gustavus Vassa.*

Norbert Rillieux (1806-1894)

Mr. Rillieux was born in New Orleans, Louisiana, on March 17, 1806. His parents were hardworking people. His dad

was a wealthy French engineer, and his mom was a plantation slave woman.

As a young man, Mr. Rillieux was given his freedom and went to Paris to study engineering at a place called L'Ecole Centrale. When he was twenty-four, he became a professor there, specializing in steam engine technology.

Mr. Rillieux designed a "multiple effect vacuum pan" evaporator that improved the quality of sugar and produced it at a lower cost. His idea was so fancy it's hard to explain.

Elijah McCoy (1843-1929)

Have you ever wondered where the phrase, "the real McCoy" came from? Elijah McCoy was a great inventor. He was famous for inventing a device that would oil machinery automatically. Trains and other machines stopped every single day to be oiled, and it was a great waste of money and time. His machine saved both time and money by doing this task automatically. A lot of people tried to copy Elijah McCoy's work, but people kept demanding the original—"the real McCoy."

Edmonia Lewis (1845-1890)

Edmonia Lewis was one of the first African-Americans to be recognized as a great artist. Ms. Lewis was a very talented sculptor. People said she made stones talk. Each of her sculptures tells a story. Ms. Lewis sculpted busts of famous people who fought to end slavery. She was also a fighter for freedom. She worked with the underground railroad. Her father was African-American, and her mother was Native American. Ms. Lewis went to Rome, Italy, where she set up a studio. Edmonia Lewis died when she was forty-five years old.

Jan E. Matzeliger (1852-1888)

"Mr. Whitney, could you tell me how your cotton machine works?" Jan Matzeliger was known to ask questions about the working of different machines even when he was very young. It is no surprise he became an inventor.

Mr. Matzeliger left Dutch Guiana for the United States around 1878. He traveled to Lynn, Massachusetts, where he found a job in a shoe company. He watched men lasting (hand-sewing) leather to the soles of shoes and decided he would try to build a machine that would do the job.

Mr. Matzeliger began experimenting at night in a cheap room he had rented. He used all kinds of odds and ends to build a model of his machine, even old cigar boxes. Mr. Matzeliger took several years to complete the machine. He received a patent for his "lasting machine" on March 20, 1883. The lasting machine made 150 to 700 shoes a day instead of only 50. Mr. Matzeliger sold his patent to United Shoe Machinery Company. Because of his invention, Lynn, Massachusetts, became the shoe capital of the world.

Granville T. Woods (1856-1910)

Granville Woods is known as the black Edison. He was born in Columbus, Ohio, in 1856. At the age of ten, he ran away from school to start work. When he was sixteen years old, he moved to Missouri where he worked as a fireman and an engineer on the railroads. Then he moved to New York City and studied electrical engineering. Mr. Woods made a telephone transmitter and an electrically heated egg incubator. These are only two of the more than sixty patents credited to him. Many of his patents were sold to such companies as General Electric, Westinghouse, and Bell Telephone.

Daniel Hale Williams (1856-1931)

Daniel Hale Williams performed the first heart operation in Chicago's Provident Hospital in 1893. The victim, who was stabbed and left to die, was James Cornish. Dr. Williams actually sewed up a torn heart without the aid of drugs. When the president of the United States heard about this operation, he made Dr. Williams chief surgeon of the Freedmen's Hospital in Washington, D.C.

Dr. Williams contributed greatly to the development of surgery and medical career opportunities for black people. Concerned that there was no hospital for blacks in Chicago, Dr. Williams established the Provident Hospital and Training Association in 1891. It provided hospital care for everyone and training for black physicians and nurses.

Sarah B. Walker (1867-1919)
(Known as Madame C. J. Walker)

Madame C. J. Walker was born Sarah Breedlove in Delta, Louisiana, on December 23, 1867. Her parents were Owen and Minerva Breedlove. When she was fourteen years old, she married, but her husband died young. After he died, she worked as a washerwoman to educate their daughter.

Soon Madame Walker's hair began falling out. She tried various remedies, but nothing worked. In 1905, she came up with a formula that could be used to help hair growth. Her experiments on herself and her family were successful, so she invented more products to help the skin and hair of African-Americans. After she spent a year in preliminary work, she traveled to different places to promote her products. Madame Walker became very wealthy manufacturing and selling her products.

Madame Walker became the first African-American woman millionaire.

Sarah B. Walker, driving

Charles Henry Turner (1867-1923)

Like most boys, Charles Henry Turner was very interested in nature. He was so fascinated by ants that he would lay on the ground watching them and wondering why they did all that work and how they found their way back to the nest. His teacher told him if he wanted to know, he had to find out for himself. Charles Turner said, "I will." Later in Dr. Turner's life, he discovered that ants use the light from the sun and other producers of light to find their way home.

Dr. Turner received his doctorate from the University of Chicago in 1907. He began teaching biology and psychology at Sumner High School in 1908. He was a dedicated, outstanding, and inspiring teacher and research scientist.

Dr. Turner looked for answers to his questions during his lifetime. He became one of the great African-American scientists of his century.

Ida B. Wells (1869-1931)

Ida B. Wells is one of the first civil rights leaders. Ms. Wells had very tough parents. They were born slaves and taught Ms. Wells to be happy that she wasn't a slave. Later in Ms. Wells's life, some people were stealing African-American lands, and African-American men were being hung for crimes they did not do. Ms. Wells did not like these crimes some white people were committing, so she fought back with words. She knew words could be powerful. Ms. Wells also helped start the NAACP. She became a fighter for justice.

William Christopher Handy (1873-1958)

William Christopher Handy is known as the "Father of the Blues." When Mr. Handy was in his twenties, he traveled across the United States playing with small bands trying to earn a few dollars. His first big hit was "Memphis Blues," which started out as an election song for Edward "Boss" Crump, the mayor of Memphis. Crump cheated W. C. Handy by not paying him for his song.

Mr. Handy started the Pace and Handy Music Company. At that time, the blues were becoming popular, and his company became a success. Before this time, blues were thought of as the music of poor people. Even though he was troubled by serious eye problems and became blind, he continued to write and publish the music of black America.

Carter G. Woodson (1875-1950)

The first history lesson Carter G. Woodson learned was the history of his own family. He was born in New Canton, Virginia, on December 19, 1875. Even though Mr. Woodson's father could not read or write, he always told all his children, "It is never too late to learn."

Carter Woodson did not attend school until he was eighteen years old. He told the principal at Douglass High School, "It is never too late to learn," and he started school. Mr. Woodson learned so fast that he finished high school eighteen months later.

Mr. Woodson went to the Philippines to teach some children. He was going to teach them a song called "Come Shake the Lomboy Tree." A lomboy is a kind of plum. The children loved the song. After seeing the children so happy, Mr. Woodson decided to teach them about their own history and heroes. The children loved it, and then he got an idea to write books about African-American history. He became known as the "Father of Black History."

Bessie Coleman (1893-1926)

Bessie Coleman might have said, "Come fly with me aboard my airplane." Ms. Coleman was the first known African-American to become an aviatrix. An aviatrix is a woman pilot. Ms. Coleman was unable to get her training in the United States, so she went across the ocean to a flight training school in France. After she finished her training, she returned home to Chicago as a full-fledged pilot in 1920.

Bessie Smith (1894-1937)

Bessie Smith was known as the "Empress of the Blues." Ms. Smith sang in clubs and small southern theaters. She sang about things that gave people "the blues," things like racism, poverty, and people with broken hearts. Ms. Smith's voice was so beautiful and strong that she did not need a microphone. Her songs covered all the sadness and joy of many African-Americans.

Ms. Smith went to New York in 1923 to make her first record. She made many records after that. "Down Hearted Blues" sold more than two million copies. Many people who heard Bessie Smith sing said that she was one of the greatest blues singers to ever live.

Marian Anderson (1902-   )

Marian Anderson, a wonderful opera singer, was born in Philadelphia in 1902. She has said that she always loved music, and she showed an interest in singing from the time she was very small.

Ms. Anderson was eight years old when she began singing in the church choir. When she was twenty-two, Ms. Anderson was awarded a fellowship that paid for a year of study in Europe. She sang in Paris, and the people there thought she had a wonderful voice.

President Roosevelt's wife wanted Ms. Anderson to sing in the Metropolitan Opera House. At that time, the owners wouldn't let her just because she was black. Mrs. Roosevelt let her sing in front of the Lincoln Memorial instead. She eventually did sing at the Metropolitan Opera House and won many honors.

Marian Anderson was the first African-American woman to be an opera singer.

Althea Gibson (1927-   )

Althea Gibson set the tone for tennis in the world. She came to Wimbledon before the famous Arthur Ashe. She decided early in her years to work hard and to be the very best in women's tennis. She was aware that she would be breaking the barrier in the tennis world. She really was a famous first.

Althea Gibson grew up in New York City. She became the first African-American to win major titles in tennis. She won tournaments like the French women's singles championship in 1956

Althea Gibson

and the United States and Wimbledon singles competition in 1957 and 1958. She was also ranked number one in the world among woman players in 1957 and 1958. Althea Gibson became an international tennis star and an inspiration to others.

Wilma Rudolph (1940-   )

Imagine being crippled as a child and having to wear a leg brace to help you walk. That is what happened to Wilma Rudolph, who got polio and had to wear a leg brace. She worked hard and eventually learned to walk and run without the leg brace. Ms. Rudolph was very determined. She ran track in high school and usually won. She also played basketball. Wilma Rudolph earned a track scholarship to Tennessee State University and ran on their team. Ms. Rudolph ran in the Rome Olympic Games in 1960. She was the first African-American woman to win three Olympic medals in track. She was considered the fastest female in the world.

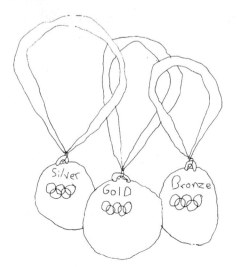

MORE FAMOUS FIRSTS AND HEROES

Here are more people who have accomplished many great things. The library is a great place to find out more on these people and many other African-Americans.

Phillis Wheatley (1753-1754)
>   First African-American poet to publish a book.

Paul Cuffee (1759-1817)
>   First African-American sea captain.

Richard Allen (1760-1831)
>   First African-American religious leader and bishop.

York (1770-1831)
>   Explorer and guide with Lewis and Clark.

James Beckworth (1778-1866)
>   Trapper in the western United States.

Lewis Temple (1800-1854)
>   Inventor of a new kind of harpoon.

Ira Aldridge (1807-1867)
>   First African-American stage actor.

Mary Fields (1832-?)
>   African-American cowgirl.

Joseph H. Rainey (1832-1887)
First African-American member of the U.S. House of Representatives.

Blanche Kelso Bruce (1841-1898)
First African-American to serve a full term in the U.S. Senate.

Nat Love (1844-1921)
Famous African-American cowboy.

Lewis Latimer (1848-1928)
Draftsman, inventor.

Henry O. Flipper (1856-1940)
First African-American to graduate from West Point.

Mary Church Terrell (1863-1954)
Women's rights activist.

Matthew A. Henson (1866-1955)
Explorer. First African-American to reach the North Pole.

Maggie Lena Walker (1867-1934)
Banker and civil rights advocate.

Oscar de Priest (1871-1951)
First African-American to be elected to the U.S. Congress in the twentieth century from a northern state.

Jack Johnson (1878-1946)
Boxer. First African-American heavyweight champion.

A. Philip Randolph (1889-1979)
Organizer of the nation's first trade union for black workers.

Paul Robeson (1898-1976)
Singer, stage actor.

Percy Lavon Julian (1899-1975)
Chemist. Found new treatment for cancer.

Charles "Chief" Anderson (1902-?)
Pilot. First African-American fighter pilot.

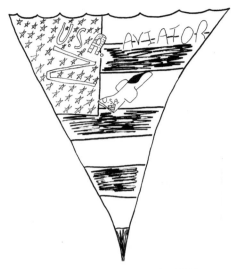

Dr. Ralph J. Bunche (1904-1971)
Diplomat, salesman. First African-American to win the Nobel Peace Prize.

William H. Hastie (1904-)
Judge. First African-American to be appointed a federal judge in the United States.

Adam Clayton Powell, Jr. (1908-1972)
First African-American to be elected to the New York City Council and strong leader for black rights.

Katherin Dunham (1910-)
Dancer, choreographer, and anthropologist.

Mahalia Jackson (1911-1972)
World-reknowned gospel singer.

Judge Berton Parsons (1911-)
Teacher, lawyer, and musician. First African-American to be appointed a federal district judge in the United States.

Jesse Owens (1913-1990)
Track Olympian. First African-American man to win three gold medals,

which he did at the Olympic
Games in Germany in 1936.

Billie Holiday (1915-1959)
Great jazz singer.

Lena Horne (1917-)
Award-winning actress and singer.

Alex Haley (1921-1992)
Author. Pulitzer Prize-winning author of *Roots*.

Constance Baker Motley (1921-)
Lawyer. The first African-American person and first woman to be elected Manhattan Borough president in New York City.

Sammy Davis, Jr. (1925-1990)
Dancer, actor, and singer. A leader who opened the door for African-Americans in the entertainment field.

Angela D. Ferguson (1925-)
Researcher for sickle cell anemia, a hospital builder, and a pediatric doctor.

Coretta Scott King (1927-)
Civil rights activist.

Carl B. Stokes (1927-)
Lawyer. First African-American mayor of Cleveland, Ohio, in 1967.

Sidney Poitier (1927-)
In 1963, he received the Academy Award for best actor for his performance in *Lillies of the Field*.

Lorraine Hansberry (1930-1965)
Playwright. Her first play, *Raisin in the Sun*, was the first play by an African-American woman to be produced on Broadway.

Toni Morrison (1931-)
Novelist. Toni Morrison's first novel, *Beloved*, won the Pulitzer Prize for Literature in 1988.

Bill Russell (1934-)
Athlete. First African-American to become a head coach in any professional sport.

Bill Cosby (1937-)
Filmmaker, teacher, actor, comedian, and author. Bill Cosby is one of today's most popular entertainment personalities.

Colin Powell (1937-)
First African-American chairman of Joint Chiefs of Staff.

Marian Wright Edelman (1939-)
Set up Children's Defense Fund.

Barbara Jordon (1939-)
Politician. Congresswoman from Texas, member of the House Judiciary Committee.

Julian Bond (1940-)
Civil rights leader and activist.

Jessie Jackson (1941-)
Minister and civil rights leader.

Muhammad Ali (1942-)
Born Cassius Clay. In 1964, he became heavyweight champion of the world.

Guion Stewart Bluford, Jr. (1942-)
Astronaut. First African-American to travel into space.

Aretha Franklin (1942-)
Singer, musician. Known as the "Queen of Soul."

Sharon Pratt Kelly (1944-)
The first black woman to be mayor of a major city, Washington, D.C.

Alice Walker (1944-)
Novelist. Wrote *The Color Purple*.

ART, MUSIC, AND DANCE

Colorful art, flowing dance,
Many people taking a chance.
Music from their very souls,
Turning dreams into goals.

In Africa, art, music, and dance are routinely used to celebrate important events in life. A birth, a death, the planting or harvesting of crops, weddings, and hunts have their own collection of rhythms, dances, and artwork. These are used to spread the news. Even if neighboring villages cannot understand each other's spoken language, they can still tell what is going on through art, music, and dance. When Africans came to the New World, they brought with them this unique tradition of rhythm, movement, and art.

In this section, we tell you a little bit about African-American culture to help you understand the music, dance, and art we enjoy today. We have included directions for you to make your own Adinkira pins, drums, and rattles. You may find names of famous artists, dancers, and musicians you will want to research.

There is enough information here to get you started. If you like this section, remember there are many, many books about art, music, and dance waiting for you in your school and public libraries.

ART

Early African Art

The oldest known African artworks are prehistoric paintings found in a mountain in the Sahara Desert. These were found on rocks, rock shelters, and cave walls, like the Egyptian hieroglyphics and modern graffiti.

African artwork includes sculptures, figures, masks, decorated boxes, and various other objects for ceremonial and everyday use. Many early sculptures were made of wood. However, since wood decays, few examples are left. Some other artworks were made of bronze, ivory, and terra-cotta (a kind of pottery). Few people outside of Africa knew about African art until the 1900s.

When the Africans were brought to the New World, they carried with them a unique art tradition. Their art showed their history, religious beliefs, and values.

Kyeke Ko Aware

Adinkira Art

There are many different African crafts. We want to tell you about Adinkira art, which is connected with the African people of central and southern Ghana and the Ivory Coast. The Adinkira are symbols that are used to decorate art and clothing. These symbols can be used to mean different things. We will give you some history of the Adinkira, along with directions for making your own Adinkira pin.

These symbols first originated from a ruler named King Adinkira who ruled Guyomen. There was a battle, and the king was killed. The Ashanti took his robe with symbols as a trophy and named the cloth after King Adinkira.

In the past, the cloth was worn to funerals as a way of saying good-bye to the dead. It is said that there are fifty-three different Adinkira symbols. The cloth is now worn at any time, not just for grief.

Adinkira pins

Look at the pictures with the symbols and their meaning. Find one that you might like to make into a pin. Here's how to make Adinkira pins.

Materials: You will need clay in many colors that will bake in a conventional oven, newsprint, pin backs or safety pins, and art glue.

1. Choose an Adinkira symbol that you want to make.
2. Get the color of clay you want.
3. Use newsprint paper when working with clay so your table doesn't turn the color of the clay. Form the clay into balls, coils, or long snakes to form your design. Mold it into the symbol using wild and wonderful colors. Be sure to leave an area large enough on the back of the symbol to attach a pin after it is baked.
4. Bake your clay on aluminum foil at 275 degrees for 20 minutes.
5. Attach a pin back to the back of the Adinkira pin with art glue. Let it dry completely.
6. Wear your pin with pride.

Dono Ntoaso

Penpamsie

Aftun Mmireku Denkyem Mmireku

Kerpa

Bi Nka Bi

Sunsum

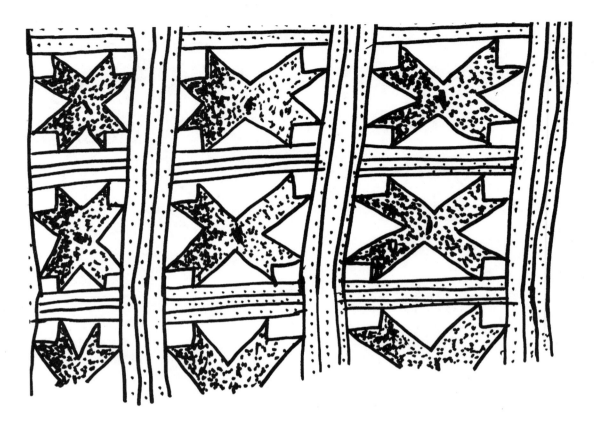

Printing Cloth

You can also print cloth using these same symbols by carving designs into potatoes and using these potatoes as stamps to print. Here's how to do it!

Materials: You will need a potato, liquid soap, tempera paint, a knife, and material or a piece of clothing.

1. Add a little bit of liquid soap to your paint for an easier cleanup.
2. Cut a potato in half width-wise.
3. Carve an Adinkira design or one of your own into the potato with a knife.
4. Stick the design side of the potato in tempera paint of any color.
5. Stamp the design on a shirt, paper, or whatever you choose.
6. Let it dry completely.

The Ashanti Africans used these designs on clothes to symbolize how they felt. Many African-Americans wear these designs on traditional clothes for special celebrations across our country.

Drums

We like the sound of drums because the sound makes us feel weird. You can make lots of sounds with them.

In Africa, drums were used to communicate long distances. Different beats, speeds, and loudness meant different

things to the listener. This custom was brought to America by slaves. Many people in America play African drums today and make beautiful music.

The drum is a percussion instrument that is played by hitting it. The body of a drum can be shaped like an open cylinder or kettle. The top is covered by a drumhead. The drumheads are made of calf skins or plastic. A cylinder-shaped drum could have two drumheads. A kettle-shaped instrument has only one. The size of the drum determines the pitch. Large drums produce deep, low sounds, and small drums have high-pitched sounds.

African musicians played drums as well as horns, flutes, lyres, and zithers. The drum is one of the oldest musical instruments in the world and had its beginnings in Africa.

Making a Drum

Materials: To make your own fantastic drum, you will need a coffee can, can opener, duct tape, colored paper, scissors, masking tape, and colorful yarn.

1. Start by removing the top and bottom from your can with the can opener. Be careful not to cut yourself. Pound down any rough edges.
2. Stretch the duct tape over one end of the can. First, place one strip across the center of the can. The second strip should be placed in the other direction to form a cross. Then add more strips that overlap each other until you cover the top of the can. Each strip of duct tape should be pulled tightly. Put a piece of tape around the edge of the can to cover the ends of the strips.
3. Cover the outside of the can with paper. Fasten the paper to the can with masking tape.

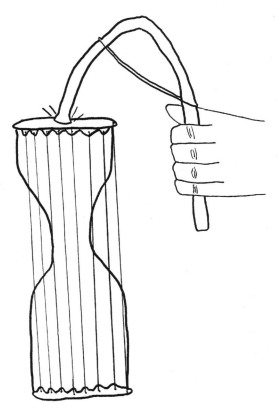

Rattles

Another ancient instrument that is fun to play is the rattle. Some dancers used rattles when they performed, and some musicians used them to accompany drums. Rattles can be made of different materials. We made our rattles using paper, but usually they are made out of gourds. Gourd seeds, such as squash, take four months to grow. The gourds are dried for about nine months. Sometimes the outside layer can be carved to make beautiful designs. Beads can be tied to the outside of the gourd to make music. This type is called a shakara. Shakaras are often covered with a hand-beaded "skirt" that adds a different sound when you shake it. Here's how we made our own rattles using paper.

4. Fasten a piece of yarn to one end of the can. Begin turning the can and covering it with yarn.
5. Push the yarn toward the top of the can with your fingers so the can is completely covered. Use different colors and textures of yarn to make your drum look great. Use a knot to tie the ends of yarn together. Put the ends of the yarn in the part of the can still to be covered. Cover the knot ends as you continue to cover the can.

Making and playing your drum is a wonderful project. Once you have finished one drum, you may want to make another so that you can experiment with the different sounds.

Making a Rattle

Materials: Use balloons, 1½-inch strips of newspaper, art glue or papier-mâché glue, rice or beans, a stick 8 inches long, tape, acrylic paint, and brushes.

1. Blow up the balloon to the size of a grapefruit and tie the end.
2. Insert a paper clip at the mouth of the balloon and tape the paper clip to the table to hold it in place. This way, it won't move while you are working on it. Later you can use the paper clip to hang the balloon up to dry.
3. Dip the 1½ strips of newspaper into the papier-mâché glue. Put the strip between your index finger and middle finger and slowly slide your fingers down the strip to remove excess glue. Do this over the bowl of glue so you don't make a mess and make your mother mad.
4. Lay a strip on the balloon. Smooth the paper flat so your rattle will look neat.

Repeat until the balloon is covered. This will take about three layers of paper. You might use plain newsprint for the second layer so you can see where you have been. Be sure and smooth out each layer.

5. Hang your balloon up by the paper clip so it can dry. This should take a day or two.
6. After your balloon has dried, remove the paper clip and without hurting the papier-mâché, poke it into the balloon to pop it. Now pull the balloon out of your rattle.
7. Use a funnel in the hole you took the balloon out of to pour the rice or beans into your rattle. As you put your rice or beans into the rattle, listen to the sound. Continue to add the rice or beans until you get the sound you like. Don't use too many beans or rice kernels, or the rattle will be too heavy, and your stick won't hold it up. Put your stick into the rattle and push in

until the stick touches the top of the inside of the rattle. Tape your stick to your rattle so that it doesn't move and the hole is completely covered.

8. Paint your rattle. Cover first with one color. When the paint is dry, decorate the rattle with Adinkira symbols (p. 45) or other designs to make it beautiful.

9. Now you are ready to make wonderful and exciting music.

African Art in the United States

Because slaves were brought from many different parts of Africa, each with a different language, the Africans in America could not talk together. Art is a form of communication that brings people together. The first Africans in America never had a chance to show their African heritage through art because the slave owners knew that this was one of their common means of communication. They feared the slaves would get together, destroy the plantation, and escape, so they discouraged it. In recent years, however, black art has been rediscovered and become very popular.

The first recorded African-American artist was Scipio Morehead in the 1700s in Boston. Even though he was living in America, he painted in the European style. There were more black artists during this time, but a lot of their

art done by slaves were not signed, you may have an authentic piece of slave art in your home and not even know it.

There was a very popular art form among white Americans showing blacks as clowns and fools. Blacks appeared eating watermelons, as Aunt Jemima, or as entertainers and minstrels. They all had black faces and big pink lips. These art forms were used as commercials for products such as Czar's Baking Powder and Dixon's Stove Polish.

These images were examples of stereotypes that show blacks as being slow, lazy, dumb, and childish. Some of these stereotypes are still around today. People pass these negative thoughts on to other people, when really everyone should be left to get to know people for themselves.

There were some black and white artists who showed blacks as they really are. They painted blacks in family, spiri-

work was lost. Some black artwork done by slaves had a practical use such as brass locks, hinges, bureaus and other furniture, rugs, egg baskets, cooking utensils, wooden banisters, and many tools. Peter Simmons, born a slave, made beautiful iron gates that still hang today. Dolls for white children were made by a slave named Emmaline.

Blacks with talent did artwork to buy their freedom. They were coach makers, sign painters, silversmiths, shipmakers, ornament makers, and quilters. An example of this is in Sidney Lanier's home, where there are quilts done by slaves showing the "log cabin" and "fan pattern" designs. Because the works of

Dolls made for white children by a slave named Emmaline

Mural at Mitchell Elementary School in Denver, Colorado

tual, work, and church settings. These artists showed blacks with dignity, class, and style. People stood posed gracefully with strength and intelligence. Unfortunately, until recently, few black artists earned enough money to support their families and themselves, because themes such as slavery, sharecropping, or ghetto life had not been known as good money-makers by leading art dealers.

In the nineteenth century, African-American artists were better documented. Some of them are Robert Duncanson, William Simpson, Edward Bannister, Joshua Johnston, Douglass Bowser, Edmonia Lewis, Henry Tanner, William Harper, and Meta Warwick Fuller. These artists used the styles that were popular in Europe. Later on, blacks started to do more works that reflected their own black heritage instead of European heritage and history.

Early in the twentieth century, Harlem, an area of New York City, became the center of a tremendous amount of creative art done by black artists. Black culture began to be recognized, accepted, and appreciated by whites. This caused the desegregation of New York theaters and provided an outlet for African-Americans to create a variety of art forms. This became known as the Harlem Renaissance.

During the depression, many black artists were employed by the Works Progress Administration (WPA). They had many jobs, one of which was painting murals. Some of their murals can still be seen across the country, from New York to Los Angeles. In the 1950s and 1960s, the type of art done by individual black artists searching for black identity consisted of murals depicting street and ghetto life painted in places like Chicago and Detroit. Another form of wall art called graffiti was started in large cities by youth of every culture. Graffiti began by being painted secretly on walls in public places such as subways or building sides. This kind of art became a competition between youth. They painted on walls or over other people's graffiti and tried not to get caught. In New York, much graffiti became well-known works of art on the subway trains and even appeared in art galleries. Some cities now have specific places where graffiti can be painted legally.

If you and your family are traveling, you may want to visit an African-American art museum in another part of the country. Some well-known museums are:

Washington, D.C.
   The Museum of African Art
   Smith Mason Gallery Museum
   (African-American and Caribbean artwork)
Chicago, Illinois
   DuSable Museum
New York, New York
   Acts of Art Gallery
   Studio Museum in Harlem
Brooklyn, New York
   The New Muse

You can look in your Yellow Pages directory for the African-American museum nearest you, or call your local art museum for information on African-American exhibits.

Here are some more black artists that you may want to do some further research on:

Benny Andrews (1930 -   )
   A famous folk artist and sculptor. He is also one of the best collage artists.
Elizabeth Catlett-Mora (1919-   )
   A sculptor and print maker. She has works in more than a dozen museums and galleries.
Barbara Chase-Riboud (1939-   )
   A famous sculptor doing shows around the world.
Ed Dwight (1930 -   )
   A bronze sculptor in Denver, Colorado. He is gaining nationwide recognition for his work.

For example, while working in a field, someone would start a song, and others would answer until everyone joined in. The people were very creative and made up the songs on the spot. They sang about things like pain, agony, and death. They also sang about love, justice, and mercy. The slaves had nothing but their belief in God, and so they sang about that a lot. If you visited a slave gathering, you would probably hear them singing songs that would reach right down into your soul.

The slaves were not permitted by their owners to get together because they thought they might plan to get away. The only reason they could meet was to celebrate their belief in God. One of the songs they sang which came from Africa was "Kumbaya," in which they asked God to "come by here."

MUSIC

The various types of music we are going to tell about all come from African-American heritage. This is just a brief introduction to these forms of music.

Spirituals

Spirituals, the earliest African-American music, were brought from Africa. In Africa, people had music and special rhythms for everything they did. In America, the slaves did not have fancy instruments, so they used anything they could find. They used their music as a form of communication—calling out their message and then having others answer them.

African-Americans also sang songs about freedom and escaping that were disguised as spirituals. There was a ship called *Jesus* that helped slaves get away. When they wanted to tell people to run away, they would sing "Steal Away to Jesus." They also sang "Down by the Riverside" to tell people where to go to escape. Other songs that sent messages were "Get on Board, Little Children" and "The Old Ship of Zion." In this song, the words are, "'Tis the old ship of Zion. It has landed many a thousand. Get on board, get on board." The slaves understood the message, and many escaped. Many of the spirituals have been printed in church songbooks, but they don't give credit to the slaves. They call them American folk songs or traditional songs. Next time you hear a spiritual, see if you can figure out the special coded message the slaves were sending to their friends.

Development of Modern African-American Music

Singers in later years changed the rhythm and style of these songs and developed gospel, blues, jazz, rock and roll, and country music. Dr. Thomas Dorsey wrote "Precious Lord, Take My Hand" when his wife and only child died. This is considered one of the first gospel songs. Now, you almost never have a funeral in the black community without that song. It has almost become a theme song for many funerals today.

Gospel music is loved by everyone. People like the emotional part that speaks to their soul. The songs talk about the feeling between yourself and your God. The songs are never in strict time and are very free-form. People clap their hands and tap their feet to the music. You sing gospel music the way you feel it. Many black musicians have not been formally trained, so they play by ear. They follow the singer and make beautiful music.

The early rural church in the South did not have many instruments, sometimes only a tambourine. The voice was used as an instrument. Sometimes singers competed with each other to see who could sing highest or lowest. The congregation also sang about how they felt. Everyone sang together in rhythm and made beautiful music.

Ragtime music is very happy and bouncy. It has a melody that consists of quick abbreviated notes. It was called "stepping music" because a person could step to the beat. It was first heard at the turn of the century, but it became even more popular in the 1970s. Only a handful of people wrote ragtime songs, or "rags," as they were called. A good place to hear ragtime is in the movie *The Sting*.

Jazz is a combination of ragtime and blues. It can be either bright and cheery or low and sad, or all of those in the same song. Jazz can come to you from out of nowhere. It is unpredictable, which means you don't know what to expect next. Jazz is very complicated because it uses more rhythms, instruments, and vocals. Jazz started with only instruments. Then words were put to the music. There is a basic melody, and then the players start adding their own ideas to expand on the original music.

The blues is another spin-off of the spiritual. Most of its themes are about love and the good and bad feelings a person has. It is sung for the public, so it doesn't have religious words. Blues songs are sometimes real slow paced and use a lot of guitar chords. The words to the songs are the most important part. The singer can change them as he or she goes along. The people in a blues audience feel the emotions of the performer. They respond by saying, "Yeah," "Tell it like it is," or "That's right."

The newest African-American music, rap, started way back in Africa. In African tribes, "men of words," or rappers, told stories and shared their wisdom with their audiences. Rap is a verbal communication using lyrics that rhyme to express a story. The chants and background music are directly related to African chants and rhythms. Some of the dances used with rap come from dances performed by warriors and are inspired by the beat of the drum, just like those of the Zulu warriors when marching off to war.

Rap is everywhere. It is so popular that young people can recite rhyming lyrics without preparation at speeds up to 200 to 250 words per minute. It has influenced the way people dress, speak, dance, and behave.

There are different kinds of rap styles. Like other forms of music, rap has its bad points. Some of the rappers rap about crime, drugs, and sex. This style is known as ghetto or hard core rap. Recordings of this kind of rap have warnings on the labels telling about the bad stuff in it.

Rap has become a new communication between people. It expresses the rapper's thoughts and relationship with society. Many times people can relate to the lyrics and find comfort or satisfaction by listening to rap music.

All the music we have written about comes from the slave experience. Even through the hard times, African-Americans gave much to the arts. A lot of the styles and rhythms that we find so exciting and new today began in Africa and were brought to us by the first Africans who arrived in America. All American music is indebted to these people for giving us a feeling that can't be defined. It is called "soul."

If you want to learn more about African-American performers, you might do more research on the following people:

Louis Armstrong (1900-1971)

Sang and played the cornet and trumpet.

James Brown (1934-   )

"Godfather of Soul." Rock and roll singer and dancer.

Duke Ellington (1899-1974)

Band leader.

Aretha Franklin (1942-   )

"Queen of Soul," blues singer.

Billie Holiday (1915-1959)

Rhythm and blues and jazz singer.

Ferdinand "Jelly Roll" Morton (1890-1941)

Piano player—claimed that he had "invented jazz in 1902."

Diana Ross (1944-   )

Singer, formed the group called The Supremes.

Scott Joplin (1868-1917)

Famous composer of ragtime.

Jimi Hendrix (1942-1970)

A rock singer and famous guitar player (considered by some to be the greatest guitarist of all time).

Richard "Little Richard" Penniman (1932-   )

Popular rock and roll singer who inspired Elvis Presley, the Beatles, the Rolling Stones, and Prince, among others.

Leontyne Price (1927-   )

First African-American to sing opera on television.

Charley Pride (1938-   )

First black to enjoy a successful country-western music career.

DANCE

African dance has influenced many of the American dances we do today. From the cakewalk to break dancing, we can trace the movements back to their roots in Africa. Most dancing was done in a single line, in two parallel lines, or in a circle. The dancers listened to the sounds of the drums and moved to the beat. Since each drum played a different beat, some dancers would have different parts of their bodies following different rhythms.

In America, slave owners often wouldn't let slaves dance. So, they would go into the woods at night to do African dances without being seen. The capoeira (COP-o-ye-da) is a dance that looks like karate. It has sharp kicking motions. It is actually a dance the slaves used to practice to help protect themselves. It is still performed every day in Bahia, Brazil.

Some people call tap dancing an American folk dance, but it really came from African tribes who pounded the earth with their bare feet. They used their heels to tap out rhythms on sun-baked clay. On the way to America, the slaves were forced to dance aboard the ships to exercise. Even then, people knew you needed to exercise to stay healthy and strong. The Africans used the foot-stomping rhythms and mixed them with the dances of the sailors. In the New World, they did the same thing on the floors of their huts or the boards of their dancing floors.

Later, metal "taps" were put on the heels and toes of the dancer's shoes to make noise. Tap dancers now use many different steps like the shuffle, buffalo, ball-change, softshoe, and continental. These are combined with clapping, slides, and props to create great sights, sounds, and rhythms. Bill "Bojangles" Robinson, Sammy Davis, Jr., and brothers Gregory Hines and Maurice Hines have all contributed to the very American style of tap dancing that is popular today.

The slaves did many dances that included placing buckets or glasses of water on their heads to show balancing skills. In the cakewalk, couples made up steps to go with the quick, short beats of the music. They had to dance along a straight path without letting the water

spill. Later on, the couple that did the best job would be given a cake. The cakewalk is still used all across America as a fun contest at church or community parties but usually without the glass of water.

Sometimes people made up dances by trying to move like an animal. The camel walk was a dance in which people tried to imitate the camel's walk. It was done by bending one knee in a jerky motion while putting the opposite heel down. A dancer who is good at it will look just like a camel walking. The dancers also did dances called the turkey trot, fish tail, and mosquito dance. In the 1960s, young people did "the monkey."

The black bottom was a dance that was introduced in 1924. It later became popular as the Charleston. It was based on a black challenge dance in which dancers tried to outdo each other. During part of the dance, the dancers slapped their backsides while hopping forward and backward.

In recent times, another challenge dance was born. Break dancing started in the inner cities. Some kids used this kind of dancing as a form of competition that doesn't involve actually fighting or hurting each other. The dancers move and spin very fast and bend their bodies in many different ways. Break dancing is usually done by young boys and men. The faster the dancer goes and the more different ways he moves, the better people like his dance. Break dancing is very difficult, and it is easy to get hurt doing it, but it is exciting and fun to watch.

A nice thing about dance is that it is always changing to go along with new music that becomes popular. African-American dance styles influenced rock and roll even in its early years. Chubby Checker introduced a Haitian dance, the Coye, when he came out with his now-famous song, "The Twist." Rock and roll is a melting pot of African-American gospel and rhythm and blues music as well as country and western. Black America had people singing and dancing to the twist, hully gully, mashed potato, watusi, and the swim.

From Africa to the present day, black people have used dance as a way to express their feelings and experi-ences. Even now, on many of the dance floors in America, you see traditional movements from Africa.

Remember there are many fun ways to learn more about dance. You might find out if your community has a cultural center that teaches African-American dances. You could also attend an African-American celebration to watch or take part in dancing. The local library will also have many books on African-American dance.

Here are some African-American dancers that you might want to look up:

Alvin Ailey (1931-   )

Formed the Alvin Ailey Ameri-can Dance Theatre.

Talley Beatty (1923 -   )
Best known for his work in musical comedies and the minstrel ballet.

Katherine Dunham (1910 -   )
Studied dances from Jamaica and served as a dancer and choreographer in motion pictures and musicals.

Gregory Hines (1946 -   )
Known for his dancing and acting abilities.

Judith Jamison (1943 -   )
Co-director of the Alvin Ailey American Dance Theatre.

Arthur Mitchell (1934 -   )
First black principal dancer for the New York City Ballet.

Pearl Primus (1919 -   )
Performed a collection of dances based on African movements.

Bill Robinson (1878-1949)
Better known as "Bojangles," considered the most famous black tap dancer.

As we leave this section of our book, we want to remember the creative energy and the talent for improvisation that African-Americans have added to America's art, music, and dance. Their style has been copied by others and, although still their own, has become truly a part of our American heritage. Music, dance, and art are wonderful gifts that African-Americans have given and continue to give to our country.

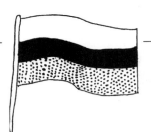

FUN, FOOD, AND CELEBRATIONS

As you turn the pages you will see,
Many good things and new recipes.
Celebrations are such fun,
With food and games for everyone.

CELEBRATIONS

Celebrations can happen anywhere, any place, at any time, and for any reason. We want to share some African-American celebrations, both national and regional, which bring African-Americans together. The celebrations you will learn about are Juneteenth, Junkanoo, Kwanzaa, and Harambee. Our nation also has holidays to honor Martin Luther King, Jr., and Malcolm X and a month to celebrate black history.

We will share recipes and ideas for social gatherings where people get together and have fun. At parties like this, people eat delicious food, dance, and listen to cool music. Taking part in an African-American celebration helps you learn history and culture in a happy way.

Freedom Celebrations

African-Americans throughout the United States have various kinds of Freedom Day celebrations to recognize the emancipation (freedom) of their ancestors from slavery. These freedom celebrations are held on different dates in different areas of the country, depending on when slaves were freed in that region. Slaves were freed at different times because news of the emancipation traveled slowly. Things like fax machines, television, and telephones were not yet invented. Also, some of the former slave owners had to be forced by the Union

Army to follow the Emancipation Proclamation.

January 1 is one of the most common dates for African-Americans to celebrate freedom, because the foreign slave trade was officially forbidden in America on that date in 1801. Also, President Lincoln declared the Emancipation Proclamation was to be followed as of January 1, 1863.

Emancipation Day is called "Juneteenth" in Kansas, Texas, and parts of the Southwest. It is celebrated on June 19. On this day in 1865, a Union general arrived in Galveston, Texas, and read a government order freeing all the slaves in East Texas.

African-Americans in Washington, D.C., have two Freedom Day celebrations. They celebrate Juneteenth on the Saturday closest to June 19, and they also celebrate it on April 16, the day slavery was abolished in the District of Columbia in 1862.

There are many other dates of Freedom Day celebrations. Some are in May, August, February, and October. For example, Jerry Rescue Day is a freedom celebration held in Syracuse, New York, which began on October 1, 1851. On this date a group of white citizens in Syracuse freed a slave named Jerry and sent him to live in freedom in Canada. The exact historical events surrounding some of the dates are not known. The people who are celebrating simply know that their ancestors were freed on that date.

When people celebrate Juneteenth or Emancipation Day, there are parades, speeches, carnivals, prayers, sermons, readings of the Emancipation Proclamation, singing, bazaars, and picnics. The Washington, D.C., Juneteenth celebration, which is sponsored by the Anacostia Museum at the Smithsonian Institution, even includes a play on Harriet Tubman and the underground railroad. No matter where or when it is celebrated, Juneteenth is a holiday that brings back the memories of slavery, celebrates freedom, and promotes the traditions of Africa.

If you want to find out about a Freedom Day celebration, you can call the local library or an African-American newspaper. Attend one. You will have fun!

Junkanoo

During the time of slavery, a tradition known as Junkanoo was started by the Bahamians (native people of the Bahamas). Black slaves were brought from the Bahamas to present-day Miami to work on a railroad. This was hard labor in the swamplands of Florida.

At Christmas time, the black slaves in this area were kept very busy doing work to prepare for the slave masters' Christmas celebration. It wasn't until the day after Christmas that the black slaves were allowed to begin their own Christmas celebration. This celebration from the day after Christmas until New Year's Day was called Junkanoo. It is a very special holiday that must be prepared for months in advance.

The highlight of Junkanoo is a competition between various bands. The members of the bands play whistles and drums and wear fancy, colorful costumes. The competition between bands is fierce, and often the different bands will go off to a secret place six months before Junkanoo to work on their costumes and music. On Junkanoo, the bands parade and prizes are awarded to the most colorful and elaborate bands. The Junkanoo parades are similar to the Mardi Gras parades in New Orleans.

Today Junkanoo is still celebrated in the Bahamas. In Jamaica it is called O'Mass, and in Trinidad it is called Carnival. It is also celebrated in Miami, Florida.

Kwanzaa

Have you ever been to a Kwanzaa celebration? Kwanzaa is a unique African-American holiday that comes from African tradition. Kwanzaa is a word for the first fruits of the harvest, and the name is actually taken from the East

African word *Kiswahila*. Kwanzaa is celebrated in the wintertime during the week of December 26 through January 1. It has similar traditions like Thanksgiving, Christmas, and Hanukkah all rolled into one.

During this celebration time, some people decorate their houses in black, green, and red and fly the African flag. In the flag, black is for the color of their skin, green is for the land, and red is for the blood they have shed. Some people may think that Kwanzaa is a religious holiday, but it really is not. It is a cultural celebration.

In the spirit of Kwanzaa, women wear a lappa or bubba, which is a name for an African dress. Men and boys wear dashikis (dah-SHEE-kees) or kanzus (can-SHOOS). They are traditional dresses for African men. They wear kofis on their heads and beads around their necks.

Kwanzaa is based on seven principles. These principles are self-determination, unity, collective work and responsibility, cooperative economics, purpose, creativity, and faith.

On the night before the last day of Kwanzaa, children give presents to their parents which remind them of Africa or their African-American ancestors. Children earn their own presents by keeping their promises from the past year. They do not eat from sunrise to sunset, but in the evening, they all gather around and feast. To us, and many others, Kwanzaa is a very strong African-American tradition.

Honoring Black History

In cities across our nation, there are different and exciting things going on in February. This is because February is Black History month. Many museums and centers across the United States plan events and celebrations that focus on African-American heritage. For example, the Denver Museum of Natural History sponsors an African-American cultural program. People are allowed to play African musical instruments and touch some everyday objects that are put in the exhibit area. There are art demonstrations and African dancers and drummers as well.

Go to your local library or your African-American history museum for more information about the events in your area.

Honoring Martin Luther King, Jr.

Martin Luther King, Jr., played a great part in history. We recognize him as an outstanding man who helped others to realize racism and prejudice are wrong. When Dr. King was little, he wondered why he couldn't sit by his white friends on the bus or couldn't drink out of the same drinking fountain. As he got older he tried to make people understand that black and white are the same. He also said, "Judge people by the content of their character and not the color of their skin." This means a lot to us because we believe that you should not judge people by the color of their skin.

After Martin Luther King's death, the third Monday in January was set

aside for people to celebrate his hard work and dedication with speeches and parades. We hope that people will remember him every day by respecting others and not judging others by the color of their skin.

Honoring Malcolm X

Some communities across the United States set aside a special day to remember Malcolm X. One of these is his hometown, Omaha, Nebraska. Every year on March 19, Malcolm X's birthday, there are celebrations and parades down main street in Omaha. Malcolm X was an African-American leader who spoke out angrily against segregation and unfair treatment of black people in the 1950s and 1960s.

Harambee

In October 1974, citizens in the African-American community of Dallas, Texas, decided to organize a celebration called Harambee. The celebration was designed to be a safer alternative to Halloween. The people also felt that Halloween didn't really have much significance for African-Americans.

Harambee is a celebration of African-American culture. Harambee is a Swahili (East African language) word meaning unity, or "let's pull together." The Harambee celebration is held at the Martin Luther King Memorial Center in Dallas every October. At the celebration, there are African-American art exhibits, films, dance and theater shows, and authentic African foods.

In 1974, the first year that the Harambee celebration was held, over 3,000 people of all ages, backgrounds, and races participated, and the celebration has grown every year! The Harambee celebration has really lived up to its name and has pulled the Dallas community together. Harambee is a positive, safe celebration that allows people to experience African-American culture.

Traditional Gatherings of Friends and Family

Many years ago, after a hard day's work in the field, the slaves would join friends in singing spirituals and toe tapping. Now, as it was back then, it is still fun to spend the weekend getting together and going to church after working all week. Saturday night fish fries are still popular today because people can talk, share, and feast.

A big tradition all across America is the family reunion. Many African-American families have reunions where family members from different states come to be together. Family reunions remind us of Sunday dinner when we go to our grandma's house and she fixes soul food

like you will find next. We eat many delicious foods like fried chicken, greens, cornbread, black-eyed peas, ribs, and catfish.

Funerals also bring family members together. People eat tasty food while sharing good memories of the person who has died.

These family gatherings are traditional to all cultures in America, but one of the secret ingredients in an African-American celebration is traditional food.

FOODS

At first, African-American foods were prepared in many ways. Meat was smoked in a smokehouse to make sure it wouldn't spoil. (Remember, there were no freezers or refrigerators at that time.) Drinks were made from the juices of fruits. Meats were barbecued, roasted, boiled, or made into stews. Vegetables were boiled or fried. Feathered wildlife was prepared by frying, baking, roasting, making broths, or simmering to form gravies. In the rivers and streams, there were a lot of fish and other water life that could be eaten. Meals were cooked in open fires using black kettles or were barbecued in open pits. The people who cooked just knew how to do it. They didn't need to follow a recipe.

The slaves were often forced to eat the scraps that the slave masters did not want. They turned these scraps into delicious stick-to-the-rib dishes. Some of these foods are black-eyed peas, cornbread, bread pudding, greens, sweet potato pie, and chitlins.

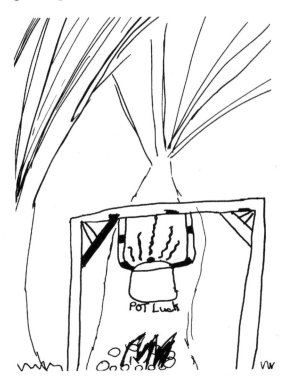

From this tradition came many mouth-watering African-American foods. You will learn about some ways African-Americans grew, cooked, and seasoned their food and their beliefs about what certain foods could do.

You might like to cook some of these African-American foods. Come on, treat yourself and try to make some of these wonderful new dishes!

Herbs

Black people brought herbs from Africa to America. Herbs are plants that grow in the ground or on a tree. They can be dried and stored to season foods later and make them taste better. They also make foods smell better. Some examples of herbs are dill, parsley, and sage. Slaves planted the herbs in a little garden on a patch of land by the slave house.

African-Americans also used the herbs to impress their slave masters, so they could go into the kitchen and cook for their family. If they were asked to

cook for the family, they might be treated better.

In the earlier days when slaves were delivering babies, they would use herbs to stop infection and help the mother. Herbs can also be used to do many other things. For example, you could drink the sassafras herb to clean your blood.

Mint is a type of herb that we had in our workshop, and we used three different kinds. They are peppermint, spearmint, and catnip. We tasted peppermint, and it was our favorite. Spearmint is an awfully good mint, too. Catnip was okay. Some liked it. However, some didn't like drinking the catnip tea because cats like to play in catnip plants. They didn't want to drink something cats played in.

Making tea the old-fashioned way is fun. When we tasted the mint tea, we couldn't believe how wonderful it was. It is fun to have on a hot summer day when you need refreshment! Just add ice and you have a nice cool drink and good breath, too! We all know how important this is to us older kids.

Fresh Mint Tea
> 1/4 pound fresh mint leaves
> 2 quarts cold water

Place the mint in cheesecloth and tie with a string. Then place the package into water in a large pan and cover. Bring to a boil, turn the fire low, and let sit for 30 minutes. Sweeten to taste and serve hot. You may also serve this tea over ice with a garnish of fresh mint and lemon.

Sassafras Tea
> 3 ounces sassafras bark
> 3 quarts cold water

Place the sassafras leaves in cheesecloth and tie with a string. Place the leaves in a large container, add cold water, and bring to a boil. Then cover and simmer for 20 to 30 minutes, depending on how strong you like it. Serve hot after you add sugar to taste. You may also serve it over ice. Many older people prefer it hot.

Biscuits

Here is an interesting "biscuit" story about Mary McLeod Bethune, the founder of the National Council of

Mary McLeod Bethune giving out diplomas. She founded the National Council of Negro Women and Bethune-Cookman College.

Negro Women. Once when she was on a train trip, they put her in a place for blacks only. The conductor said, "Auntie, do you make good biscuits?" This made her very angry because out of respect she should have been called Miss or Mrs., not Auntie. She said, "I am an adviser to the president. I am an organizer and founder of the National Council of Negro Women. I am a leader among women! And . . . I make good biscuits!"

We used the following recipe.

Down-Home Biscuits

    2 cups all-purpose flour
    1 tablespoon baking powder
    1 teaspoon salt
    1/3 cup shortening or 1/3 cup
    cooking oil
    3/4 cup milk

Combine flour, baking powder, and salt in a large bowl. Cut shortening into flour mixture until it forms coarse crumbs. Add milk. Mix with fork until particles cling together. Form dough into a ball and transfer to lightly floured bread board. Knead gently 8 to 10 times. Roll dough out with rolling pin until about 1/2-inch thick. Cut with 2-inch round cutter or cut into 2-inch squares. Place on baking sheet. Bake at 400 degrees for about 15 minutes.

To make shortcake, add 1 cup sugar. Then prepare the filling and topping. Wash and prepare 2 pints of strawberries. Top with milk, cream, or whipped cream. (Heritage Recipe from *The Black Family Reunion Cookbook* by the National Council Of Negro Women.)

Cornmeal

Cornmeal is an important part of the African-American diet. There are many ways to use cornmeal. You can fry it to make fritters, or you can bake it to make cornbread. You can even make corn sticks and corn muffins using cornmeal.

Our cornbread was great. It was golden yellow and tasted sweet and delicious. Cornbread is a fast and easy dish to make when you're in a hurry. It is fun to make, tastes great with greens, and is easy for little brothers and sisters to cook.

Cornbread
  1½ cups cornmeal
  3/4 cup flour
  2½ teaspoons baking powder
  1/2 teaspoon salt
  1¼ cups buttermilk
  2 eggs
  2 tablespoons oil

Grease a 9-inch pan with oil. Mix all ingredients in a bowl. Pour mixture into the pan and bake in the oven at 425 degrees for 18 minutes.

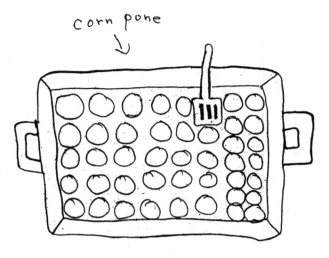

Corn pone

Corn Pone
  1 cup flour
  1 cup yellow cornmeal
  1/2 teaspoon salt
  1 egg
  1 cup milk (optional use water)
  2 teaspoons baking powder

Heat skillet, add 1½ tablespoons cooking oil until hot enough that a drop of batter bubbles immediately. Mix flour, cornmeal, salt, egg, and milk or water until smooth with no lumps. Place a spoonful in 4 or 5 places in a hot skillet. Let brown and turn over like a pancake and brown on the other side. Serve with butter and honey.

Black-Eyed Peas

Black-eyed peas came from Africa. They are a healthy food that people eat to become strong. The black-eyed pea is very tasty and has to be grown in a hot climate. Today they grow in the Deep South. Some African-American people believe that if you eat black-eyed peas on New Year's Day, you will have good luck for the new year. I am going to try this next year! It will be fun.

Mom's Black-eyed Peas
- 1 pound black-eyed peas
- 4 cups water
- 1 medium onion
- 1/2 teaspoon salt
- 1/4 teaspoon pepper
- 1 cup cubed ham (optional substitutes: 2 polish sausages, 2 hot sausage links or bacon)
- 1/4 teaspoon dried red pepper (optional)

Pick and wash black-eyed peas. Place in slow cooker or a large Dutch oven if you wish to cook them on the top of the stove. Combine with salt, pepper, onion, water, and ham or other meat. You can add crushed red pepper if you like spicy food. Simmer on the top of the stove or turn crock pot to high and allow peas to cook 3 to 4 hours. Serves 6 to 8.

Greens

Does your mom make you eat spinach? In our workshop, we ate greens. Boy, were they good! Greens are vegetable leaves and are very tasty. The basic greens are collards, mustard greens, and turnip greens. There are so many different kinds you can't count them all! In

some states such as Kansas, you can pick wild greens such as dandelions, poke salad, and wild lettuce.

Hundreds of years ago when people were slaves, they planted greens in a little piece of land their owners gave them. Some slaves cooked greens in an iron pot. If you were making a "mess of greens," you were cooking a lot of leaves, water, and meat in a big black pot or any kind of pot.

The really great part of cooking greens is the liquid that is called "pot likker." This is the juice from the vegetables, meat, and leaves when it is cooked. We think it is the best part of all! It is healthy for you if you drain the fat off the meat before you add it to the greens. The flavors are mixed together and really taste good. You can drink it, pour it on top of cornbread, or save it and put it in the freezer to season the greens the next time you cook some. Here's our recipe for greens.

Home Greens
> 2 bunches turnip greens
> 2 bunches mustard greens
> 1/2 pound salt pork
> 1/2 pound of bacon (sliced or cubed)
> 1/2 teaspoon salt
> 1/2 teaspoon pepper
> 2 dried red peppers
> 1/2 medium onion chopped

Place greens in cold water with one teaspoon of salt. Let set for about 10 minutes. Wash greens. Put in plain cold water, picking out any pieces that are bruised or broken. Break off all very large stems. Make sure you wash greens thoroughly so they are cleansed of any sand or soil. In a large pan, fry meat until browned. Drain off fat, if you prefer a healthier meal. Add greens, water, and seasoning, and cover and cook for 1½ hours on low heat or until greens are tender. Use juice with greens and cornbread.

Peanuts

On a cold winter night in the Ozark mountains, George Washington Carver, then a tiny baby, was traded for a race horse worth $300. We think he was a real bargain. Dr. George Washington Carver is the king of the peanut, "The Peanut Wizard." There are hundreds of products discovered by Dr. Carver from the peanut. He used the peanut to make face powder, printer's ink, and soap, to name just a few. He was a wonderful scientist, and he experimented with many things.

We made many things from peanuts, including peanut butter, peanut butter balls, banana peanut butter sandwiches, and vegetable peanut butter sandwiches.

We think you should know something about peanuts before you cook with them. Peanuts grow well in Georgia, Alabama, North Carolina, Texas, and Virginia. They grow underground like a potato. You can eat peanuts many different ways. Peanuts have different names, like goobers, goober peas, ground peas, and pindas. We met a special teacher who does shows on the goober, which is an African name for the peanut. People call this teacher Mrs. Goober, and you can read about her in the Real People section. Mrs. Goober helped us make these things.

Peanut Butter

  2 cups peanuts
  1½ tablespoons sunflower or
     peanut oil

Use a blender or food processor to grind the peanuts. Use a smaller blade if you want finer-ground peanuts. Use bowls to catch the peanuts as they are ground.

Place 1/4 cup peanuts and 1 tablespoon oil in blender or grinder. Blend at high speed for 10 to 15 seconds. Slow motor and continue to grind for about 45 more seconds. Use a spatula to remove from blender. If peanut butter is too dry, add more oil. Spread on crackers and serve immediately. Store leftover peanut butter in an airtight jar in the refrigerator.

Peanut Butter Banana Sandwich

  1 teaspoon orange juice
  2 tablespoons peanut butter
  2 sliced bananas
  4 slices brown or natural grain
    bread

Add juice to peanut butter and mix until thinned. Spread thinned peanut butter on the bread. Top with banana slices. Cut in halves or quarters and serve.

Vegetable Peanut Butter Sandwiches

  1 tablespoon mayonnaise
  2 tablespoons grated carrots
  2 large crisp lettuce leaves
  3 tablespoons peanut butter
  1 tablespoon diced olives
  1 tablespoon diced green peppers
  4 slices bread (white or wheat,
    your choice)

Mix mayonnaise, carrots, olives, and peppers together with peanut butter. Spread on bread, top with lettuce leaf. Cut in 1/2 or 1/4 pieces. Serve immediately.

Other additions for good healthy peanut butter sandwiches are:
  toasted pumpkin seeds
  sunflower seeds
  pickles (sweet or dill)
  cream cheese
  raisins
  cucumbers

Bread Pudding

In the olden days, people could not afford to throw anything away. If they had a lot of leftover old bread (the bread that was made with flour, not cornmeal), they would crumble it and save it. The whole message behind bread pudding is people could not afford to waste or throw away food, so they recycled it. People back then used everything. With bread pudding, they used the stale bread to make a delicious dessert. Here's how we did it:

> 4 cups dried bread crumbs
> 2 eggs beaten
> 2 cups milk
> 1/2 cup sugar

1/2 teaspoon vanilla
1/8 teaspoon cinnamon
1/8 teaspoon nutmeg
2 tablespoons butter
1½ cups raisins

Mix all the above ingredients. Place in 350 degree oven. Bake for 45 minutes or until the center is firm to the touch. Can be served hot or cold.

Sweet Potato Pie

We sure liked eating sweet potato pie. A lot of people have pumpkin pie for Thanksgiving, but you can have sweet potato pie instead. This pie is made of yams or sweet potatoes and is really popular in the South. It's delicious! This is what you need.

2 cups cooked mashed sweet potatoes
1⅓ cups sugar (brown or white)
1 teaspoon vanilla extract
1 teaspoon lemon extract
1 teaspoon cinnamon
1/2 teaspoon nutmeg
3 eggs
1/2 cup milk or half and half
3/4 stick of butter

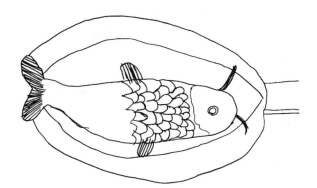

Peel and cube sweet potatoes.
Mash potatoes with all the above ingredients. Beat on medium speed of mixer
until smooth, or you can mix it until
your arm gets tired. Place in pie shell.
Bake at 350 degrees for about an hour or
until firm when touched in the middle.

Catfish

Catfish can be cooked different ways—
frying, barbecuing, baking, and any
other way you can think of. When we
have cookouts, a lot of people come
over. We have barbecued catfish. Fish
fries are used as a special time for family
and friends to get together. Our catfish
had a spicy, delicious flavor. It was fun
making this recipe. Ask your mom or
dad to help you fry catfish for the family
dinner. You need to be careful because
this recipe is fried in hot oil.

Fried Catfish Strips
    1 catfish fillet
    3/4 cup cornmeal
    1/2 teaspoon salt
    1/2 teaspoon pepper
    1 cup cooking oil

Take the fish fillets and cut into
bite-size pieces or little strips. Mix cornmeal, salt, and pepper together. You can
season it the way you want by adding
some other spices to this mixture. Heat
oil to 350 degrees in an electric skillet.
Cook on one side until it is golden
brown. Turn it over until the other side
is brown, too. Lay the fish on a paper
towel to soak up the extra oil.

"Soul" Ice Cream

Many people enjoy eating ice cream in
the summer. It's more fun in the summer
because you can take your old-fashioned
ice cream freezer outside, make your
own ice cream, and cool off. You turn
the handle until the ice cream is frozen.
You can also take turns with your friends
and family. When the ice cream is hard,
take the dasher (this is the beater) out.
It's great fun to lick. This is our way to
make ice cream. Some people use electric freezers. The ice cream tastes just as
good, but it's not as much fun to make.

1 cup heavy cream

1 cup light cream

1/2 cup sugar

3/4 teaspoon vanilla (optional, can be lemon, nuts, fruit, or other flavors)

Pinch of salt

Makes 2 quarts

Using a wooden or plastic spoon, stir contents until sugar dissolves. Place this mixture in an ice cream container. Insert dasher. Place the lid on, and be sure it is snapped or screwed firmly in place. Lock support arm firmly in place. Plug in, if freezer is electric. Have ice and salt ready. Layer ice-salt-ice-salt around the container. As the salt melts the ice, continue to replace it. Freezing time is 20 to 50 minutes. Use your plastic or rubber spatula when stirring in your container, so you do not damage interior or dasher. When ice cream reaches consistency you like, remove dasher and serve immediately or store in the freezer until ready to serve.

Emancipation Proclamation Snackin' Cake

Our special African-American cook gave us this wonderful recipe for an easy cake. This cake is called a snackin' cake because you can fix it fast, anytime you want, and eat it as a snack.

1/2 cup butter

1 cup sugar

2 eggs

2/3 cup milk

2½ cups flour (sifted)

3 teaspoons baking powder

1/4 teaspoon salt

1 teaspoon vanilla extract

Cream butter, add sugar gradually, blend well. Beat eggs well and add to butter and sugar mixture. Mix sifted flour, salt, and baking powder. Add milk a little at a time. Finally, add vanilla. Use two 9" x 12" buttered cake pans. Bake for 30 minutes at 375 degrees.

We hope you try some of these recipes and celebrations. We found them all very exciting. Remember to look around your community for the celebrations they have. This is such a fun and delicious way to learn about the African-American heritage.

STORIES, LANGUAGE, AND LITERATURE

As you read these stories,
You will find,
Laughter, sadness, hope,
And fun of all kinds.

STORIES

When Africans were brought to America as slaves, almost everything was taken away from them. But the slave owners could not take away their rich tradition of storytelling or their imaginations. Slaves were forbidden to speak their native languages and to write, but they continued to tell stories. Some stories were based on memories, while others were based on new experiences and hopes.

Animals were often the heroes in African folktales. These heroes showed up again in this country in the stories told by slaves. The African jackal became the American fox, the African hare became the American rabbit, and the African tortoise became the American turtle. In some stories, animals and young children were made to be smart and strong because slave masters did not let the slaves show their intelligence. "Brer Rabbit" and "Wiley and the Hairy Man" are examples of this kind of cleverness.

Animals were also used to answer questions about nature. "How the Turtle Got Marks on Its Shell," "How the Sea Creatures Found Their Home," and "Why Spiders Have No Hair" are just a few examples.

The stories told in slave cabins, around campfires, or in underground hideouts did more than entertain. "The

People Could Fly" and "Follow the Drinking Gourd" had hidden messages telling slaves how to escape, how to hide, and who would help them. They were also a good way to teach morals. "The Talking Eggs" shows the importance of following directions and being respectful.

These stories were told from one generation to the next, and they passed along history, culture, hopes, and fears. African-American culture grew and expanded through these stories. The stories are so interesting that they can be enjoyed by both children and adults.

"Brer Rabbit Gets Brer Fox's Dinner"

One day Brer Rabbit was walking down the road by Brer Fox's house. Brer Fox was putting new shingles on his roof. In the yard was Brer Fox's dinner. Brer Rabbit knew that there was more food in the basket than in his own stomach. He couldn't beat Brer Fox in a fight, so he'd have to think of another way to get that dinner.

Brer Rabbit said, "Hey, Brer Fox, what are you doing?" Brer Fox answered, "I'm putting new shingles on my roof."

Brer Rabbit asked, "Can I help?"

Brer Fox said, "OK, but I'm not sure you'll be much help."

Brer Rabbit started to hammer nails into the shingles. He was fast. In no time the roof was finished. Fox screamed, "Rabbit, unnail my tail!"

Rabbit said, "Gee, I've never nailed a tail before." As he was climbing down the

ladder, he muttered, "I must be losing my aim, my stroke, or something, or maybe my eyesight is getting weak. How could I have nailed his tail? Making a mistake like that always makes me hungry."

While Brer Fox continued to holler, a grinning Brer Rabbit enjoyed a fine dinner.

"Wiley and the Hairy Man"

One day a long time ago, a boy named Wiley was sent to gather sticks by the Tombigbee River, in Alabama. His mom said, "Take your hound dogs because the Hairy Man will get you if you don't."

When he got to the Tombigbee River, his hound dogs ran off to chase a rabbit. A minute later the Hairy Man came. Wiley climbed up a tree. The Hairy Man took an ax out of his bag and started chopping down the tree. Wiley said, "Fly chips fly, fly back to your own places." And the wood chips flew back into place. The Hairy Man chopped faster. Wiley yelled louder, but the Hairy

Man was winning. Then Wiley heard his dogs barking. He called them, and they chased the Hairy Man back to the swamp.

Wiley was scared, but his mother said, "Next time, tie up the dogs. Tell him that you know he is the best magician around." So he tied up the dogs. Soon he saw the Hairy Man coming through the trees swinging a sack. The Hairy Man was smiling because he knew Wiley had lost his dogs. Wiley wanted to run; he was scared stiff. Wiley said, "Hello, Hairy Man, I hear you're the best magician around here."

"I know," said the Hairy Man.

"I bet you can't turn yourself into a gorilla," said Wiley.

"Sure I can," said the Hairy Man, and he did.

Wiley said, "I bet you can't turn into a lion."

"Oh yeah?" said the Hairy Man, and he did.

Wiley said, "Anybody can turn big. Bet you can't turn into a mouse!"

"Oh yeah?" said the Hairy Man, and he did it.

Then Wiley picked him up and threw him in the bag and threw the bag in the river. Wiley felt happy, but he knew the Hairy Man would come back.

"You fooled the Hairy Man two times," said his mother. "If we fool him three times, he will never come back." Wiley was too nervous to sit still. Outside he tied up one hound in the front and the other in the back. He built a fire while his mother sat down to think.

Wiley's mom made him bring her a young pig from the pen. She put the pig in Wiley's bed and had Wiley hide in the loft.

Wiley heard the Hairy Man climbing up onto the roof. He tried to go down the chimney but couldn't because it was hot. Then the Hairy Man jumped down, knocked on the door, and asked for Wiley. Wiley's mom said, "You can't have him, Hairy Man." The Hairy Man thought of a couple more tricks to try to get Wiley, but every time his mother outsmarted him.

Finally, Wiley's mom said, "If I do give you the young'un, will you go away?" The Hairy Man swore he would.

When the Hairy Man got to the bed and pulled back the covers, all he found was a young pig. "I never said which young'un I'd give you," Wiley's mom said.

Then the Hairy Man huffed and puffed and cursed, gritting his teeth, as he went away with the young pig. Wiley and his mother had fooled the Hairy Man three times. Now he would never come back.

"How the Turtle Got Marks on Its Shell"

One day a turtle was out with his wife. They were so poor and hungry. The turtle said, "Today is the town's marketing day. We shall buy some food."

The turtle's wife knew they had no money. She hoped that some day she and her husband could get food. She then noticed her husband admiring several eagles flying around.

Her husband said, "I wish that I could eat as often as those eagles."

The eagles overheard him and said, "We would be happy to carry you to our king up in the clouds. He will feed you."

The turtle, filled with joy, accepted and was taken high in the air, forgetting to invite his wife.

The turtle asked, "Who is the food for?"

One eagle replied, "For everyone."

The turtle, supposedly very wise, said, "Let us all choose names for ourselves."

While the turtle chose the name "Everyone," the eagles chose human names.

When the eagles and the turtle were on the clouds, the king eagle came out with bowls of wonderful fruits and meats. Turtle also noticed all sorts of other foods.

The turtle cried out, "Who is the food for?"

The king said, "For everyone."

The turtle then claimed all the food because his name was Everyone.

When the turtle was done eating, he said, "Fly down to my wife and tell her to lay down some soft things for me to land on when I fall from here."

The eagles did just the opposite because the turtle had been so greedy. They told her to put down broken bottles, rocks, and all sorts of hard things.

When the turtle jumped down, he hit his shell on all the glass and rocks. That is how the turtle got marks on its shell. Turtles have marks on their shells even today, as a reminder of the turtle's greediness.

"How the Sea Creatures Found Their New Home"

Many years ago in the forest, sea creatures wandered around on the land. There were fish, octopuses, sea horses, and eels, but they didn't have a home or a place to call their own. They went in search of a new home with their leader, the King Blue Whale.

The creatures packed their things and walked and walked and walked until they came to a beautiful yellow land. They wanted to stay there. One Octopus said, "This land is beautiful!"

The Sea Horses said, "Is this our new home?"

They were resting in the new land when a mean lion came. He roared at them and told them to leave. This land was his, and he wasn't going to share it with any sea creatures.

The King Blue Whale told them to be patient. The animals walked and walked and walked until they found another beautiful place. The King Blue Whale said, "This land is be-yoooo-ti-ful!"

The Sea Horses said, "Is this our new home?"

This was pretty, green land. The Whale looked around, but just as he was about to say "Yes," he heard a horrible, loud, awful screeching noise. A great gray elephant lumbered up. "What are you creatures doing here?" he demanded, swinging his long gray trunk.

"We are looking for a new land," answered the King Blue Whale.

"Well, you cannot stay here. This is my home, the land of the Elephants. You must move on."

The Fish said, "Where are we going to live now?"

The creatures packed up their things again, and they walked and they walked and they walked. The Eels asked, "How much farther do we have to go?"

The creatures walked and walked and walked. By this time they were so tired, they were losing their legs. The Eels asked again, "How much farther do we have to go?" They looked around. This blue land was beautiful. It was quiet. There was no lion and no elephant. Now they were not walking *on* the land, they were floating through it. It was water.

The Sea Horses asked, "Is this our new home?"

The King Blue Whale looked around. He looked left. He looked right. He looked up. He looked down. Then he grinned a big whale grin. "Yes!" he said. "This is our land and will always be our land." And so the Sea Creatures had found their new home—the ocean.

"Why Spiders Have No Hair"

Anansi the spider lived in a village in Africa. He was a show-off. He liked people to think that he was the best. When his mother-in-law died, he wanted to act sadder than anyone else. He decided not to eat for eight days. Anansi knew he would get hungry, so before he went to the funeral he stuffed his face. After the funeral, his family had a feast, but he refused to eat anything. He said, "I say what I mean and I mean what I say. I will not eat until the eighth day."

On the third day, his family went out into the field to gather food. They left Anansi in charge of the large pot of cooking beans. He was so hungry he couldn't take it anymore. He took a big cupful of hot beans. Just when he was going to take a bite, he saw his family coming back. He had to hide the beans fast, so he dumped them into his hat and put it back on. The beans were hot on his head, so he started to shake his hat. When his family saw him, they asked

what was wrong. As an excuse he said, "In my village, today is the hat-shaking festival so I'm shaking my hat. I think I should go join them."

He started to leave, still dancing and shaking his hat, but his family followed him so that they could join in the festival, too. When he couldn't take the hot beans on his head anymore, he threw off his hat. His family picked it up and saw the hot beans. They started laughing.

Anansi jumped into the tall grass to hide himself. That's why spiders hide in tall grass and have no hair on their heads.

"The People Could Fly"

The slaves were seasick and sad coming to America. They were forced to work on plantations, which were owned by their white masters. Even though they had to give up their freedom, they still had their imaginations. They told stories of faith and hope.

Once a woman, called Sarah, was beaten to the ground; she couldn't get up. Her baby cried, so it was whipped by the driver. If the slaves didn't work hard and fast, they were beaten until they bled. A wise magic man, called Toby, said magic words to help the slaves fly to freedom. Only the strong could fly. Only those who had faith in their ability to escape could fly.

Toby said, "Kum ya li kum buba tambe," and these words made them fly. The slaves forgot their native language because they weren't allowed to speak

it, but they still remembered enough to make them fly.

The owners tried to beat down the flying slaves, but it didn't work. Toby followed the flying slaves. He was magic, and he was God's helper. The slave driver wanted to kill Toby, but he couldn't. Toby laughed at him and said, "We are the ones who fly!"

Not all of the slaves flew, because they didn't have enough faith. The people who couldn't fly told their children about the people who could.

* * * * *

Flying in this story has two meanings. Strong faith (flying) helped the slaves be free in spirit even when they were working. It also took strong faith to "fly" or escape to freedom. This story offers hope that all people can be free and respected.

"Follow the Drinking Gourd"

During the time of slavery, stories had hidden messages to help slaves escape.

Peg Leg Joe and other legendary underground railroad conductors worked as handymen for different plantation owners. At night they would teach the slaves a story that gave directions for escaping. The slaves began singing this story, "Follow the Drinking Gourd." Here are some of the words to the song: "Follow the drinking gourd / The riverbank makes a very good road / The dead trees will show you the way / Left foot, peg foot, traveling on / The river ends between two hills / There's another river on the other side / When the great big river meets the little river, follow the drinking gourd. / For the old man is a-waiting for to carry you to freedom if you follow the drinking gourd."

Many versions of this story have been written down. All of them agree on the following facts. The drinking gourd referred to the Big Dipper, which pointed to the North Star and the way to freedom. Escaping slaves were warned to travel by river. They looked for a footprint and a peg print on dead trees that marked the path. The Tombigbee River, which starts in Alabama, was the "river that ends between two hills." Next they would come to "the river on the other side," or the Tennessee River.

As their journey continued, they would meet the old man waiting to carry them to freedom at the great big river. If they made it that far, Peg Leg Joe or another helper would escort them across the Ohio River, into the free states and to an underground railroad station. These stations were often houses or barns with secret rooms to hide the escaping slaves.

Their journey was still dangerous and frightening until they were able to cross Lake Erie into Canada. Anywhere along the way they could have been caught and returned to their owners. Once in Canada, they were really free.

"The Talking Eggs"

Way before you were born, there was a shabby house in the woods. An old woman lived there with her two daughters, Blanche and Rose. Blanche was as sweet as sugar, very generous and always willing to help around the house. Rose was terribly spoiled and thought only of herself. She was also very greedy and stingy. Their mother liked Rose best because she and Rose were so much alike. They were very mean to Blanche and made her do all the work around the house. Rose and her mother always dreamed of going to the city to be grand ladies.

On a hot day the mother sent Blanche to the well to get water because Rose was thirsty. After filling the bucket, Blanche saw an old woman in a deep

black shawl. The woman asked kindly for a sip of water. Blanche, being very kind, said "Yes, ma'am." So as to repay Blanche's kindness, the old woman invited her to her shack to spend the night and have dinner. The old woman made Blanche promise not to laugh at anything she saw at her house.

The first thing Blanche saw was a two-headed cow with corkscrews for horns. She also saw chickens of all colors with different numbers of legs. Strangest of all, they whistled instead of clucked. Although these things were strange, Blanche kept her promise and did not laugh at any of it.

While they were inside, the old woman asked Blanche to light a fire and start supper. All there was to put in the pot of water was an old beef bone, which magically turned into stew. The old woman also gave Blanche one grain of rice, which turned into many grains of rice as soon as it was ground. Just when Blanche thought nothing could be stranger, the old woman took off her head and started braiding her hair. When she finished, she put her head back on. Then they sat on the porch and watched grandly dressed rabbits dance and play music on the front lawn.

The next morning Blanche went to milk the two-headed cow, which gave her the sweetest-tasting milk. Next she collected the eggs. The old woman had told her to collect only those eggs that said "Take me" but to leave the ones that said "Don't take me." As it turned out, the ones that said "Don't take me" were jeweled and colorful. The ones that said "Take me" were just plain white eggs. Blanche was tempted to take the pretty ones, but she obeyed the old woman.

The old woman promised Blanche, as she was leaving, that things would get better. She told her to throw the eggs over her left shoulder one at a time as she walked home. Each time she did this, wonderful things came out of the eggs. The eggs became beautiful dresses, shoes, diamonds, rubies, and even a horse and carriage.

When Blanche got home with all her newfound riches, her mother and sister were very jealous—so jealous, in fact, that after questioning Blanche, her mother sent Rose off to find the old woman and get more.

Rose found the old woman, but things did not turn out the same. Rose laughed at the strange animals, refused to cook, received sour milk from the cow, and took the eggs that said "Don't take me." All of this led to her downfall.

On her way home, each time she threw an egg over her right shoulder, something terrible came out. She tried running home, but the snakes, lizards, and wolves followed her. Her mom heard her yelling and tried to save her, but the animals chased them both into the woods.

When they finally made it back home, Blanche had left for the city to become a grand lady. She remained as kind and loving as always.

The moral of this story is: It pays to respect people's differences and not make fun of them.

LANGUAGE

Language is a very powerful tool. Slave owners hoped to keep slaves powerless by outlawing their African languages. White owners believed that if the slaves only spoke English, they could not make secret plans. At the same time, slaves were severely punished for speaking "formal" English. They were accused of learning to read or being "uppity."

To not appear "uppity," they developed their own language system and sentence structure. Black English also grew out of the need to communicate without the white community being able to understand. Blacks combined both African and American words to form codes and passwords. When slaves spoke to each other the white master heard one thing, but the slaves often meant something else.

Black English is still spoken today, but many African-Americans think it is important to be bilingual. Black English is used around peers, family members, and within the black community. Formal English is used at school and at work.

Many expressions and sayings have been passed from one generation to the next. Some, originally considered black slang, are now common in mainstream America. How often do you use the word "OK"? It originated from the African word *Yaw Kay*. When Elijah McCoy's industrial machine was being copied, customers began asking for "the real McCoy." This meant that they wanted the original, not an imitation. See how many of the following expressions you recognize.

Words with African Origins

African	Afro-American	Meaning
Hipi	Hip	Aware
Cat	Cat	Person
Goy	Guy	A young man
Dega	Dig	Understand
Tota	Tote	Carry

Black English Phrases

Someone done gone on	Someone has died
Get yo' piece of paper	Get a diploma
You put yo foot in that!	You cooked a great meal!
You actin like Miss Ann	You think you are better than others
Pick that lip up	Stop pouting
I like to died!	I was shocked (happy or sad)
I declare!	An expression of surprise
That tickled me	That made me laugh
You are being seditty	You are acting fake
Run my mouth	I talk a lot
Talk that talk	Give compliments, joke or flirt
That ain't even down the song	That's not the way it happened
Mamma din' raise no fool	Do not think I am ignorant
Jive	Cool talk
Only go pieca way	Part of the way
A hard head makes a soft behind	Not listening will cause you trouble in the future
Grub	Delicious
Chill (out)	Calm down
Scarf	Stuff food or overeat
Dibbies	I saw or claimed that first
What's up Duke?	What are you up to?
He be, she be	He is or she is
She foyine (fine)	That's an attractive person
Livin' large	Living well
Check dis	Pay attention; listen
To cop	To get
Check it out	Look at this
Jammin	Having big fun
G	Refers to a friend or peer
Word!	Said to agree enthusiastically
Funna	Means going to do something
Digits	Phone numbers
'Sup?	What's going on?
How you livin?	How are you?

LITERATURE

While much African-American history is still passed down orally, it is also being written down. Slaves sometimes risked their lives to learn to write. It was the narratives of escaped slaves that helped others work to stop slavery. Many black authors are being published in the twentieth century. Their work records all aspects of African-American life. These are just a few of the outstanding books by African-American authors who appeal to large audiences and have earned awards for literary achievement. Look for these and other books at your local bookstore or library.

Roots: The Saga of an American Family by Alex Haley (New York: Doubleday & Company, Inc., 1976). This is a story about an African warrior and his family before, during, and after the time of slavery. People liked the book so much that they made it into a really long television movie.

Roll of Thunder, Hear my Cry by Mildred D. Taylor (New York: Dial Books, 1976). This moving story shares the struggles of a young African-American girl as she grows up.

Fallen Angels by Walter Dean Myers (New York: Scholastic Inc., 1988). Mr. Myers wrote this book in memory of his brother who died in Vietnam.

Mufaro's Beautiful Daughters by John Steptoe, illustrated by John Steptoe (New York: Lothrop, Lee & Shepard Books, 1987). This is a story of two beautiful daughters competing to be queen.

Nathaniel Talking by Eloise Greenfield, illustrated by Jan Spivey Gilchrist (New York: Black Butterfly Children's Books, 1988). This book is about a kid named Nathaniel and his rap poems.

Aunt Flossie's Hats by Elizabeth Fitzgerald Howard, paintings by James Ransome (New York: Clarion Books, 1991). A grandmother tells her grandchildren a story from her childhood.

REAL PEOPLE

Ministers, artists, and lots of others,
Children, fathers, sisters, and brothers.
The more they say, the more you learn.
It takes all people to make the world turn.

We are very proud of this section. We feel it has some of the most important information in the entire book. It is important because it comes from real people, people just like you and me. They come from neighborhoods, schools, homes, places, and experiences that are the same as yours and mine. They have been generous enough to answer a list of our questions plus tell us even more than we could have hoped. They share with us their life stories as well as their values and goals, providing information that you can't generally find in books. This information comes from the heart and soul.

The real people that you will read about have two main things in common. One, they are African-American, and two, they never gave up. When they ran into a problem, they persisted until they overcame it.

Although these people are of different backgrounds and have different occupations and are from different parts of the country, you will find a common thread running through their lives. Their parents stressed education as a high priority. Families and a belief in God are also a key to success.

We hope you will learn a lot about them and enjoy them as much as we have.

DARYL PRICE

Daryl Price is 6 feet 5 inches tall and weighs 254 pounds. He plays outside linebacker. Because he was quite talented when he played football for a high school in Beaumont, Texas, he was recruited to play for the University of Colorado Buffs and has an athletic scholarship. Even though Mr. Price has a chance to make a career in football, he feels his education is more important to him than his athletic career. If he was to get hurt, his football career could be over. Therefore, his main goal is to receive degrees in molecular biology and religious studies.

Daryl Price was born on October 23, 1972, in Galveston, Texas. He has two younger brothers, aged 11 and 13, and an older sister, 21. He recalls always having a full house to deal with because his cousins often came to stay with them.

Mr. Price feels that education is the key to fighting racial discrimination. When asked about prejudice, he said, "I get mad at the thing [the discriminatory act], not at the person. I try to learn more because I don't want people to have the idea that African-Americans can't learn or aren't intelligent. The media contributes to putting people in these categories."

Mr. Price looks up to Martin Luther King, Jr., because he believed in something and stuck with it right to his death. Mr. Price tries to apply this to himself. At one point, he was going through some particularly tough times. He began to wonder why he didn't seem smart. Then

he met this very intelligent African-American girl who was ranked second in their class. From that point on, Daryl Price decided you can't use being black as an excuse, and you have to decide what you're going to do and do it.

When Mr. Price was growing up, his parents weren't always able to visit school, go to awards night, or go to his games. It's not that they didn't care, but they just didn't have the time. They worked all day and all night to pay their bills and to clothe and feed their children. One thing his family taught him was there is always a right way and a wrong way. Even if it might take longer to do something the right way, it's better than doing something the wrong way. The family always spent Sundays together and attended church.

Daryl's best advice for young people is, first, to trust in God. Second, get an education and don't let people tell you what you can or cannot accomplish. Daryl Price is an African-American willing to do what he's got to do to get where he needs to be.

DOROTHY JENKINS FIELDS

"It is important for African-American youth to study and explore the history of their heritage. With this knowledge they can work on the problems of today to make a better world."

On New Year's Eve, 1942, Dorothy Jenkins Fields was born in Miami, Florida. Her grandparents had moved to Miami from the Bahamas in 1903. She was an only child with lots of cousins. As a little girl, she loved to listen to her two aunts and four uncles while they entertained her grandmother with jokes and family stories. Mrs. Fields's mother inspired her to strive to do the best she could. She sums it up by saying, "My mother is the wind beneath my wings."

During the 1940s, African-Americans were called "colored" people. As Mrs. Fields grew up, they became known as "Negroes." In the late 1960s, some people began calling themselves "black." Still later, blacks started to choose what they wanted to be called. In the 1970s, the name changed to "Afro-American," but today, most people use the title "African-American." Dorothy Jenkins Fields believes it is important to be able to choose a name for yourself and not have others tell you who you are. She calls herself Afro-American.

Mrs. Fields is married and has two daughters, Katherine and Edda. Katherine is a graduate of Spelman College and is studying for her master's degree in Business Administration. Edda is a senior at Emory University studying in Sierra Leone, West Africa.

When it comes to food, Mrs. Fields loves to eat, especially when someone else does the cooking for her. Family birthdays are celebrated with parties and friends, and the entire family takes pride in sending birthday cards to a large circle of friends.

One day Mrs. Fields went to the library to read about local African-Americans. The clerk told her they only had a folder with obituaries, which are notices of people who have died. When Mrs. Fields asked why, the clerk said, "I guess those people have not thought enough of themselves to write their history." Mrs. Fields disagreed and realized the need to collect and organize information so that books could be written about African-Americans in Miami. She hopes to develop a program in which African-American youths become actively involved in recording their own ethnic heritage and sharing it with others.

Mrs. Fields started the black archives in Miami. An archive is a place to keep important papers. Because Mrs. Fields runs the archives, she is called an archivist. The archives she started contain the histories and important papers of people in Miami's black community. They also have reference books, architectural drawings, oral history tapes, sound recordings, exhibits, slides, videotapes, and newspapers.

Miami is very fortunate to have the talented Dorothy Jenkins Fields, a social studies specialist and archivist in the Dade County Public Schools, helping African-American people understand their heritage and live a better life.

LEON SMITH

Leon Smith is an African-American who has dedicated twenty-six years of his life to the military. Mr. Smith represents a large number of African-Americans who have served our country in war and peace. He believes that the most important things in his life are bonding with his family and getting a good education. Mr. Smith's family, like many others, contains mixed heritages. One of his grandfathers was part Irish, and another was Cherokee and grew up on an Indian reservation in Oklahoma.

As a child, Mr. Smith's favorite role model was Nat King Cole, because he wanted to be a singer. He has two younger brothers and one older sister, and he loves his family very much.

Mr. Smith was born on January 30, 1928, in Maple Hill, Kansas. The town only had 208 people in it. Church played a very big role in his family life, and they had to walk four miles every Sunday to attend. At school he got good grades but was often teased because he was one of the only African-American kids there.

Mr. Smith has done many things in his life. He has been a singer, been in the army for three wars, and worked as a hotel cook. His truck battalion was first to enter Berlin in the Second World War. They went through "the Berlin Corridor," which he said was a very scary situation. He was very troubled by the way African-Americans were treated in the service. They fought and died beside the white soldiers every day but were separated in their living quarters until a 1949 law forced the military to integrate. He fought in an artillery unit in the Korean War. Mr. Smith also fought in the Vietnam War.

Mr. Smith was very active in the Baptist church, even when he lived in

different countries around the world. When he was a soldier in Korea, he helped a missionary. They worked in a leper colony. Normally, no one was allowed to visit in leper colonies, but Mr. Smith did.

A person who stands out in Mr. Smith's mind as being very special was Mr. Krammer, a white man. Mr. Krammer gave him his first job as a fry cook and always treated him fairly. Mr. Krammer was like a father to him.

Mr. Smith feels that school helped him achieve success. Education was very important to him. His wife was also very important in his life. When she died at the age of forty-five, he raised his three girls and two boys alone. Mr. Smith feels that parents are models for children, and he has tried to teach his children the importance of religion, responsibility, and education. He said, "Families stay together and work together." He feels blessed with eight grandchildren. Family celebrations stand out in his memories, especially Christmas, Thanksgiving, New Year's, and the Fourth of July (his sister's birthday).

Being an African-American growing up in small towns in Kansas, Mr. Smith remembered prejudice being called "Jim Crow." Whenever he was teased, he walked away and ignored his teaser rather than fight. As a child, his brothers and sister helped him to solve problems in other ways than fighting. When they were young, they liked to dance. They danced on a small platform outside of the dance hall. They weren't allowed to dance with the white people. Prejudice was very strong when he was growing up.

Mr. Smith's feelings of equality are very strong. He feels many jobs are not given to blacks even though they are very qualified.

Today Mr. Smith is retired from the army. He keeps active taking care of his grandchildren. Mr. Smith said if he could change one thing in the world, it would be to have more education about different cultures in the school system. This way, people would see that they are all equal.

GEORGETTE AJULUFOH

Georgette Ajulufoh is an African-American who sees her people as smart and strong. As a bright, young woman engineer, she thinks African-Americans must educate themselves if they are to do well in life. She would also like to help educate other African-Americans and start her own company someday.

Mrs. Ajulufoh, born in Jackson, Mississippi, July 29, 1963, is an example of what a good family can provide. She is the product of a good education and excellent role models. Her parents were strict but loving and a strong influence in her life. They taught her to live by the Bible, to treat people equally, to get a good education, and to have high moral standards. They also taught her how to behave, because they knew this would represent them.

As an independent-minded woman, Mrs. Ajulufoh has made two major deci-

sions in her young life. One was to leave home after graduating from college, and the other was to get married. She decided to leave Mississippi so she could be on her own. Her husband is from Nigeria, a country in Africa. Before she met him, she thought Africa was just like she had seen in the movies. After meeting and getting to know her husband and learning about his country and culture, she now sees that there are many similarities between his African homeland and her southern roots in the United States.

While Mrs. Ajulufoh lived on the farmlands of Mississippi, she learned that family ties are more important than anything else. She has a deep appreciation for close relationships and family values. Her father was her first hero. He was a very big and strong man. He protected his family and always showed his two daughters that life had many challenges. He died when Mrs. Ajulufoh was ten years old. Her mother then became the family's strength, working two jobs to support the family. Mrs. Mckenzie, Georgette's mother, gave her two daughters the help and encouragement they needed to be successful. Georgette became strong and independent. You can see why her parents are her role models.

As a child, Mrs. Ajulufoh and her younger sister, Phyllis, were encouraged to stay in school and to get a good education. Mrs. Ajulufoh went to Jackson State University in Mississippi and earned a B.S. degree in computer science. She now has a job as a systems engineer in Troy, Michigan, where she designs and writes computer programs for EDS, a branch of General Motors Corporation.

Mrs. Ajulufoh can remember that in seventh grade, two boys picked on her because of her color. It was a very hard time for her. She didn't want to go to school, and she could not stop the teasing. She felt very bad inside and lost much of her self-esteem. Mrs. Ajulufoh worked extra hard to prove that she was better than the people who picked on her. She thinks that people should be judged by their character or personality and not their race.

As an African-American woman, Mrs. Ajulufoh thinks she has always worked harder to prove that she is as good as the next person. She is bothered by this. If she had the chance to make a positive change for our society, she would wish for people to be color-blind. She would also like for all young African-Americans to "educate themselves." Kids should "stay in school, learn as much as they can, and be the best they can possibly be."

RANDY E. JORDAN

Randy Jordan told us that prejudice comes from fear. Fear comes from not knowing ourselves. If we teach more about our culture and learn about others' cultures, prejudice can be eliminated.

Mr. Jordan was born on October 31, 1950, and lived in the Chicago housing projects. He and three brothers and a sister were raised by their mother.

Mr. Jordan is proud to be African-American. He has been married for twenty-two years and has twin daughters who are 21 years old and a son who is 10. He has three jobs. In one, he makes computers talk to each other. In another, he writes a publication for African-Americans called *The Black Orange*. This is a paper that tells about things that are happening in Orange County, California. His third job is being a minister. He hopes to start a church where he lives in Mission Viejo, California. He tries to teach more about African-Americans in the Bible. He says there is much rich history, and this is his commitment. He feels African-American history is an important part of the Bible that is not being taught.

When Mr. Jordan was growing up in Chicago, he played football in the housing projects. Many of the homes didn't have a dad, so the men who took time to show an interest were very important people in their lives. The young boys were looking for an image from an adult male, someone they could look up to and learn to pattern their life after.

Since Mr. Jordan didn't have a dad, his uncle became very important in his life. His uncle kept him in line and gave him someone to look up to.

Thanksgiving was a special family time for him when he was growing up. It still is today. It is a time when he and his family can come together to give God thanks for all he has given to them.

During Black History month, Mr. Jordan and his family try to wear the clothes that are a part of their heritage. They wear "kente cloth" to show pride in their African-American heritage. A "kanga cap" is another item they wear. This cap for men is a square type of crown. The women wear another type of cap actually called a crown. These caps come in various colors, and wearing them shows pride and unity of African-American people. Mr. Jordan feels that kids need to know more about the clothes of their heritage.

Sometimes Mr. Jordan experienced people being mean and bad to him. They were mostly teasing him because he was African-American. Many people in his neighborhood were ashamed of their color. He learned to be proud of who he was. Mr. Jordan says this is an exciting time for African-Americans. Our moms and dads may not have had the opportunities and the education that we have. We have been given a chance to be ourselves.

Mr. Jordan would love to take away hate in our country. Hate allowed this country to almost completely destroy the Native Americans of this land. Hate has caused people to do awful things to each other. Hate keeps people from accepting what they could accept. If you try to judge before you know someone, you may be wrong. Hate has caused many problems, and all kinds of people need to work to stop it.

SYLVIA KIRK

Sylvia Kirk wants to be accepted for who she is, "a black African-American woman." Throwing textbooks out of the window so that kids can live history is what Mrs. Kirk does. She is a very intelligent and creative teacher who works in Midwest City, Oklahoma. After talking with her, we would love to have her for our teacher.

Mrs. Kirk's mother was a high school graduate. She went on to college but left college to get married. Her father was a construction worker.

After her parents divorced, Mrs. Kirk grew up in an extended family with her grandparents, mother, and cousins. The divorce affected Mrs. Kirk later on in her teens. Even though her mother remarried, she still was hurt that she did not have her real father around like other kids did. She cared for her stepfather, but he was not her real father. She grew up in New York and the Catskill Mountains in Pennsylvania. She lived in mixed neighborhoods where there were Jewish, white, and black people. She liked to go outside and jump rope, which was popular at that time. Sometimes at night her grandmother would go out on the porch and tell her stories about the past. Some of the stories were about her grandfather's experiences being a sharecropper. He leased or rented land from another person, and at the end of the year, her grandfather and his partner would split the profits of the harvested crop. Mrs. Kirk's grandmother sang old religious spirituals and spoke of hardships she had to live through. These hardships didn't bother her because she believed all people have to deal with hardships in their lives. Mrs. Kirk thought so much about this that later, when she became a teacher, she wrote a play about her grandparents' life, and her students performed it.

Her mother and grandmother worked very hard to teach Mrs. Kirk to be proud of what she is and her heritage. It wasn't until she went to school that she first discovered prejudice. She remembered that her teachers sometimes placed students in a group because of their skin color. These students didn't have a chance to study the way they wanted. Mrs. Kirk's mom was different, and she made sure that the teachers challenged her daughter.

Mrs. Kirk thinks that God and her family are the most important things in her life. At Thanksgiving, they thank God for the blessings he has given their family. These values came from her mother and grandmother who are her heroines.

Mrs. Kirk has been married over 20 years. Her husband was a major in the air force. He was a mission crew commander and worked with reconnaissance planes, which are planes that take secret pictures. They have three children. Dana is 9, Shoan is 12, and Rhyan is 14.

Mrs. Kirk believes that people should be called what they want to be called. She wants to be thought of as an African-American. She also believes that people should not think that someone is bad just because their skin is a different color. Being African-American is wonderful, although there are many difficulties because of color. People tend to lump African-Americans together, which is a disservice to them. African-Americans are a people with a rich heritage. Mrs. Kirk wishes that we had a color-blind society where all people would be treated equally.

Mrs. Kirk told us that we should try to get an education and strive for excellence. Kids should make goals so that they know where they are going and work hard to get there. She believes it is hard for people to ignore you or treat you unfairly when you are the best!

RODNEY JONES

"The soul inside of me has no color, everybody's soul has the same color."

A star, Rodney Jones, was born on August 30, 1956, in New Haven, Connecticut, to proud parents, Mary Ellen and Lawrence Jones. As a 9-year-old, he enjoyed going to Palisades Amusement Park with his father and friends. He loved the cotton candy and hot dogs. When he wasn't at the amusement park, he and his friends played hide and seek around and in the Union Theological Seminary where his father was the dean.

Mr. Jones loved his family very much. His parents taught him to have a strong sense of what is right and wrong and to believe all people are a gift from God. His father told him that words and

actions should be the same, but actions should come before words.

Mr. Jones wants to inherit his father's honesty, self-discipline, and self-control, and he also wants to be appreciated by people around him.

Mr. Jones loves to eat. Some of his favorite foods are sushi (raw fish), chicken, barbecue ribs, frozen fruit juices, and popsicles. He thinks his mom is the best cook in the world. "But, of course, everyone thinks that," said Mr. Jones.

Leana Mitchell, Serena Lynn, and Laura Alia are Mr. Jones's three loving daughters and his pride and joy. Leana wants to be a writer and teacher, and Serena and Laura want to be veterinarians when they grow up.

At a young age, Mr. Jones played in a band with a good friend, Jackie Byard. Once Mr. Jones wrote a song called "Gaze." Like other songwriters, Mr. Jones sat by the radio hoping his song would be played. After four months, he heard his song. He loves his guitar, but sometimes he plays the electric bass. Bruce Johnson, a jazz guitarist, is a good friend and a wonderful role model, teaching Mr. Jones to find the creative spark within himself. Mr. Jones now works as a music teacher at the Manhattan School of Music. He teaches music composition and gives guitar lessons.

Mr. Jones has lived his whole life through accepting and learning new things everyday. He takes things slowly but learns things very quickly. His belief in God is strong, and he prays every day.

Mr. Jones is kind and warm-hearted. He is doing something to help African-American people learn about their culture, and he wants to share his music with everyone.

BILL POTTS

Bill Potts believes people are different in many ways and are alike in many ways. He thinks all people should be treated equally and fairly.

Mr. Potts is a folk artist. He has been married for thirty-two years and lives and works in the Denver area. He was born March 22, 1936, in Des Moines, Iowa. Like many African-Americans, Mr. Potts has different heritages. His father was three-fourths Native American. His mother was an African-American. Mr. Potts can trace his family tree back to the time of slavery. His grandmother was a slave.

After earning a scholarship to Drake University, Mr. Potts dropped out in his junior year to join the army. He later served in Vietnam. He stayed in the army for twenty years. Mr. Potts was the only African-American in his platoon. When he was confronted by racial discrimination, he said he didn't let it get to him. Once when he was in the service he had to sit in the back of the bus because he was African-American. He couldn't figure out why he had to sit in the back of the bus. After all, he had paid the same amount of money as all of the other guys had.

From a very young age, Bill Potts was very artistic. As a child, he would build things out of cardboard, wood, and other scraps that he found. Today he is a folk artist who sells his carvings across the country. Mr. Potts has been married to his second wife for thirty-two years. His first wife died very young.

When Mr. Potts travels in his car, he stops and picks up wood off the side of the road. He never lets one piece of wood go to waste. He recycles and turns hunks of junk into works of art. He carves many things like animals, rocket ships, walking sticks, and people. He also enjoys going to the movies and flying his cardboard airplanes in his spare time.

Mr. Potts, a man with a strong belief in God, is following his dream to the point that he is willing to make sacrifices. He goes without a lot of extras like fancy clothes and cars because he doesn't always have the money to buy them. He gives his time and artwork to many worthy causes. He spent the entire day with us at our workshop. He gave us a fish he took the time to make right in front of our eyes. He started with four old two-by-fours that had been glued together. He used a saw to start carving the wood. We began to see the shape develop. He used the sawdust to help keep the glue together. Some of the tools that he used were a rasp, which is like a large file, many power saws, and other power tools. After we saw the shape of the fish, he painted the fish using bright red, blue, and white colors. These colors are used by many folk artists. He left this beautiful fish for us to enjoy. Each time we see it, we will remember a man who is very artistic and sincere about his work. Mr. Potts taught us to never give up on our dreams and to dedicate our time and effort to our dreams and goals. He is kind, caring, funny, and a hardworking man. Thank you, Mr. Potts. You taught us a lot.

CARNEICE BROWN WHITE

Carneice Brown White was born in Memphis, Tennessee, on June 22, 1929. Her father was a Pullman porter for the railroad, and her mother was a caterer and a homemaker. She has one older sister. When Mrs. White was young, her family lived in Memphis until she was nine years old. Then they moved to Denver, Colorado.

Carneice Brown White is married to Matthew Lee White. He is a realtor and employee of the Denver Bulk Mail Center. She has two adult children. Her son, Drusel, is a musical arranger and keyboard player. Cecilia Kay, her daughter, was the first African-American "All-American Girl." She has a son named Omar and likes to play the harp.

Mrs. White retired after being a teacher for forty years. In all those years of teaching, she has had a chance to see many changes happen for African-American children. The most exciting thing about this is that Mrs. White has not only seen change but she is usually the one who makes it happen.

After working with students for so many years, she saw that many of her inner-city students needed opportunities to experience a place where learning is fun. She wanted to teach her students how to eat in a fancy restaurant. She called the restaurant and told them what she needed. The manager of the restaurant let the kids eat free! Since the restaurant was over one hundred miles away, Mrs. White called an airline and got them to provide an airplane for the kids to ride on! This was exciting for them because many of the kids had never been in an airplane before. Mrs. White says that if you want the world to be a better place, each person has to do something. She feels that if you are willing to ask, you will find people who are willing to help you make a change. Because of her great teaching, Mrs. White was recognized as one of seven Outstanding Black Educators in America by the National Council for Negro Women.

Mrs. White helped continue a great tradition for the fifth graders at her school. Since the fifth-grade students would be leaving the elementary school to go to a junior high school the next year, she thought it was important for them to have a continuation ceremony. This is like a graduation for the fifth graders. The reason it is called a continuation ceremony is to remind the kids to

to teach all children about African-American history. She wants the children to learn about black culture in a fun way and with understanding and friendship. One of the programs Mrs. White will have at the museum will be "The Magic of Goobers." This is a program in which she dresses up as Mrs. Goober and tells children about how much African-Americans have done for the United States. She is Mrs. Goober because "goober" is another name for the peanut. The peanut came from Africa to the United States. The program is meant to build self-esteem and pride in young African-Americans. Mrs. White was awarded a grant from the Public Service Company of Colorado to promote "The Magic of Goobers" nationwide. This grant should help her reach her dream of opening the African-American children's museum.

Because Mrs. White makes time to think of ideas for change and since she has the strength to put them into action, her example has caused other people to take action. What can you do to make the world a better place? Don't forget what Mrs. White says: "If you are willing to ask, there are people willing to help."

PAUL STEWART

"You can't be a cowboy 'cause cowboys aren't black." This is what Paul Stewart heard every time he and his friends played cowboys and Indians.

Mr. Stewart is an African-American cowboy. He was born on December 18,

continue in school, to graduate from high school and maybe even college. Students dress up in their best clothes and march into the auditorium. While they are there they listen to speakers like Denver Mayor Wellington Webb who tell the kids to keep learning and to finish school.

Now that Mrs. White has retired, she is not going to sit at home. She has already made plans to start an African-American children's museum. She wants

1925, in Clinton, Iowa. His mother was three-fourths Native American. His father was African-American. His father owned a trucking company and wanted his son to be a truck driver also. Mr. Stewart's father always told him, "A winner never quits, and a quitter never wins." These are the words that he lives by today.

Through the years, Mr. Stewart was the only African-American child in his school. Growing up in the North, he never really knew the strong prejudice that African-Americans in the South did. He remembers that once his father, driving a truck down to the South, got stopped in Little Rock, Arkansas. The authorities took his dad to the police station and accused him of stealing the truck. They told him, "You can't own a truck. You are not allowed to have property." His father had to make many calls, and he finally was able to prove that the truck was his. This stuck in Mr. Stewart's mind, and his father became an excellent role model for him. He saw in his dad a person who did not let people beat him down. He never quit.

Church has also played an important role in his life. He spent a lot of time during his youth praying. After church, his family would often go on church outings. Mr. Stewart felt that these outings were important as well as fun. So it is no surprise that his minister was also a role model for him. He would often ask his minister to pray for him and give him strength.

Mr. Stewart's family is very important to him. He had one sister and two brothers. He can trace his roots to well-known author Alex Haley and famous sports figure Jesse Owens. These people show that "a winner never quits and a quitter never wins."

Mr. Stewart saw his first black cowboy when he moved to Denver. He was shocked because he never knew that there were black cowboys. He read all he could about them and collected everything he could about the West, including boots, guns, spurs, and ropes. Whenever he met an African-American cowboy, he would ask him many questions about cowboys and if he would like to donate items to his cowboy collection. During his research, Mr. Stewart came up with another role model. He found a cowboy, Jesse Stahl, who represented not only strength but creativity. Jesse Stahl would bring the rodeo crowd to their feet by riding his horse into the ring and having the horse fall on him.

The crowd would think Mr. Stahl was dead. After about five minutes, he would slide out from under the horse, get up on the horse's back, and wave to the crowd. The crowd would applaud him. In 1971, Mr. Stewart started the Black American West Museum and Heritage Center in Denver, Colorado.

Today, along with operating his museum, Mr. Stewart teaches African-American history to students everywhere. He has written two books, *Westward Soul* and *Black Cowboys*. He plans to write three more books: *Black Music, Black Mining,* and *Black Women.* Mr. Stewart has also been written up in many magazines and newspapers.

During his lifetime, Mr. Stewart has faced racism. Once, while in the service, he and a friend went into a southern town and boarded a bus. He paid his fare. His friends went directly to the back of the bus, but he stood in the front. The bus driver had to ask him to move to the back. He did not understand because he had paid the same fare. Another time, he went to get his shoes shined and sat down. All of the men doing the shining were white. Not one of them would come and help him. He also went into a soda shop for a drink. The white man showed him to the end of the counter. The African-American man who was sweeping the floor and cleaning was told to serve him. Mr. Stewart just turned to the white man and very politely said, "No, thank you," and walked out.

Mr. Stewart believes that fear is a big key to prejudice. He thinks prejudiced people do not feel good about themselves and pick on others to cover up their own bad feelings.

Mr. Stewart leaves us with this idea: Remember, to get something out of what you do, you must put yourself into it.

FATIMAH LINDA COLLIER JACKSON

Paul Laurence Dunbar said, "Life for me ain't no crystal staircase." This statement does not have a negative message for Fatimah Jackson because she believes that challenges help people become stronger. This positive attitude has made her a happy and successful person. She is what her role models, her grandmother and her mother, would have called a balanced person. Her mother and grandmother taught her to be honest and creative and never lose sight of her goals. Ms. Jackson remembers her grandmother always using leftovers to make another meal, never throwing out something useful. Later, this lesson was repeated in Ms. Jackson's Muslim belief that when there is enough food for one, there really is enough for two. This idea of sharing and sacrificing is important to Ms. Jackson's life.

Fatimah Jackson was born on September 6, 1950, in Denver, Colorado. She grew up in a large extended family with her grandparents and other relatives. Her neighborhood included many different heritages, including African-Americans, Hispanics, and Japanese-Americans. She remembers a happy

childhood but knows that segregation existed. Certain people could only live, eat, and work in certain places.

Since her father died when she was six, her mother and grandmother took care of the family. Her favorite family times were vacations in the mountains. She loved playing with her cousins and remembers running up and down hills, drinking fresh spring water, riding in the back of a truck, visiting a dairy, and tasting ice cold milk.

Ms. Jackson's present home is Adelphi, Maryland, where she lives with her husband and six children. Family holidays revolve around African-American celebrations such as Kwanzaa and the Muslim religion. One celebration is called Eid ul Adaha, the feast of Abraham, which remembers the story of Abraham and his willingness to obey God and sacrifice his only son. This celebration comes at different times of the year because Muslims use the lunar, or

moon, calendar. In 1992, the celebration is in the spring, but in 2000, it will be in the winter. Her name, Fatimah, was added when she became Muslim. She feels becoming Muslim helped her become a better person.

Ms. Jackson finished her undergraduate work at Cornell University in Ithaca, New York, and was acknowledged for excellent achievement. She majored in science and then received her master's degree and her doctorate. While writing her dissertation, a long paper she had to write to receive her degree, she traveled to Africa to gather research. Now she is a professor of biological anthropology at the University of Maryland. Her husband is also a scientist.

Ms. Jackson thinks her marriage was one of the most important decisions she made. For her it was the right choice since she has been married for over twenty years. She has six children. The two oldest are in college, and the youngest is just three. Her family is close, and they depend on one another.

The first encounter with prejudice that she remembers came in a college classroom. Ms. Jackson remembers that she felt the professor judged her by her color, not her ability. She had always been a good student, so at first she was surprised, and then she became angry. She made a point of telling her instructor early in a new semester that he would be receiving A work from her. She thinks that by turning this situation around, she gained her professor's respect and challenged herself to do her best.

Ms. Jackson bases her daily life on her religion. She tells the African-American youth of today the beliefs of her elders: believe in yourself, do the best that you can, and do everything you can to reach your goals.

The continent and people of Africa are very important to Ms. Jackson. This continent is the homeland of human life and the cradle of civilization. All people can learn from the rich history of Africa and Africans. The Quran (Koran), the Muslim Holy Book, also states that humans were created by God as different nations and tribes so that we would get to know each other, not so that we would dislike each other. This is one of many passages that guide her life.

STEVE FLOYD

Imagine a world where we meet someone we know and we become a part of each other's lives. The color of our skin doesn't make us good, but what counts is how we treat others. This is how Steve Floyd, a former gang member wants the world to be.

Steve Floyd was born on Easter Sunday, March 29, 1959, in Chicago, Illinois. He feels that being born on Easter was special, because Easter is a day of sharing and accepting everyone no matter what color they are.

Mr. Floyd grew up in a one-parent family on the south side of Chicago. He was raised in the Robert Taylor Home projects, which was one of the poorest

housing projects in the nation. He went through many hardships while he was growing up. His father had to leave his family to serve in the Vietnam War. When his father returned from Vietnam, his parents divorced. Later, his father was found dead on the street. His mother had to struggle to support Steve and his four brothers and one sister and was unable to spend much time with her children. Growing up without a father, Mr. Floyd turned to gangs for male acceptance and friendship. At age 17, he was grazed in the head with a .38 bullet by a rival gang member. He survived and decided he had enough of gang violence.

After Mr. Floyd gave up his life as a gang member, he moved on to bigger and better things. He went to college and earned a degree in theology and Bible studies. He is now the Director of Outreach and Management with At High

Risk Youth Services in Minneapolis, Minnesota. This program deals with inner-city street gangs. He feels there are better things than gang violence to get involved with because violence destroys people. He tries to motivate young people to have a better life.

Mr. Floyd thinks it is important to have friends. He knows from personal experience how strong the need to belong can be. However, he warns kids that belonging to a violent gang can be deadly. He tells kids they should remember that they always have choices. Kids need to make good choices, not bad ones. When your friends want you to do violent, bad things, you shouldn't be afraid to be your own person and do your own thing.

When asked about racial discrimination, Mr. Floyd said it was a shock to him because when he was young he lived in an all-black neighborhood and had never seen white people except on television. The first time he realized that people judged others by the color of their skin was when he rode his bike into a white neighborhood. His bike broke down, and he had to carry it out. While he was struggling to get the bike home, a white man accused him of stealing the bike and slapped him in the face.

This is a valuable lesson for all of us. Just because people look different, it doesn't mean they are doing bad things. He feels that African-American people are special and that God is looking out for them. He says that African-Americans need to understand their heritage. They need to learn to love and accept one another. They need to take pride in themselves.

Steve Floyd has three children named Steven, Chloe, and Josef. He told us that he is living for his kids first and other kids second. He believes that we need to provide many activities for youth today so they don't get into violent gangs. Our whole country needs to help solve the gang problem so our streets and neighborhoods will be safe places to live.

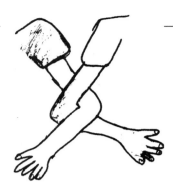

OUR VISION FOR A BETTER TOMORROW

There is a large problem in America today, one that has been around forever. We read about it in the newspaper, or friends tell us about it. It's on television, and we even see it with our own eyes. Some people choose to ignore it or pretend that it's not there. Ignoring it is just another way of letting it continue. This problem we're talking about is racism.

Racism is a whole way of looking at people. It involves a person thinking that he or she is better than another person because of religion, culture, or even something like the color of skin. This way of thinking has led to discrimination against certain people. We have all run into someone who has made fun of us or people close to us, and it hurts. Plainly,

"racism" and "discrimination" are based on things that don't really matter at all. We have to accept others for who they are. You don't have to be best friends with everyone, but give everyone a chance. This way you can find things you have in common. The more you learn about another culture, the more you can learn about yourself.

We are trying to stop racism and discrimination now. We want all kids who read this book to stop judging others by their differences. We challenge you to learn about your own heritage and share it with others in a way that shows that you are open to listening about their culture too. What we are asking for is a lot, but if you take the time, you will get to know people as they really are.

STUDENT AUTHORS

Aja Armstrong
Andra Arnold
Adrianna Baker
Katie Baker
Lizabeth T. Barnish
Jesse E. Julio Beason
LaRoy Bias
Nicole D. Bias
Adrian H. Bing
Shannon Boutwell
Bryan Brammer
Mara Jones-Branch
Kimberly L. Burnell
Ashley R. Carlson
Kirsten J. O. Carson
Benjamin C. Dallet
Jeremy N. Dillman
Brandon Dudley
Lindsey Dudley
Jacee' Louise Elbeck
Jessie Ellis
Sarita Evans
Carrie Fann
Nancee Feagans
James Fuqua
Laura Ann Fuqua
Josh Funderburg
Matthew James Gallegos
Meleaha Glapion
Thomas Glapion
Michelle Renee' Greene
Brooke Gustafson
Zach Haberler
Brittlee Hanson
Simone M. Hicks
Elisha L. Hill
Chinwuba Ikwuakor Jr.
Uzi C.B.N. Ikwuakor
Derek James
Jaquay Jenkins
Branden A. Johnson
Adrienne Jones
Andrea C. Kelly

Monticue A.C. Kimble
Jasmine M. Langford
Maurice L. Langford
Mechelle Love
Anthony B. Martin, Jr.
James E. Martin
Janell M. Martin
Starr Martin
Aaron Martinez
Alisha L. Martinez
Jacob Edras Montoya
Karree Moore
Harrison D. Nealey
Brian J. Noble
Eric T. Noble
Mark Parker
Josh J. Pettit
Karlyda R. Poindexter
Amy Marie Pomranka
David M. Poppleton
Joseph Poppleton
Brian P. Quinn
Mary Elizabeth Robinson
Cliff M. Rodriguez
Paul Ruzzo
Shaz Sedighzadeh
Christopher Smith
Megan Stenbeck
Asheber P. Swanson
Sarah-Gayle Swanson
Bernicia Thompson
Courtney Ward
Brittni West-Ware
Aisha Williams
Chad Williams
Joloni Shane Williams
Naima N. Williams
Lindsay Ann Windels
Anthony Max Wright
Cecil J.A. Wright
Jamilah Wright
Carly L. York
Charles Youssef

TEACHER PARTICIPANTS

Carneice Brown-White, African-American
  Consultant
Jean Tiran Cable, Assistant Director
Linda L. Carlson
Susan Chichester
Parke Covarrubias
Judith H. Cozzens, Director
Tom DeAngelo
Mary Ann Garcia-Pettit
Edith Glapion
Lorraine Gutierrez
Brenda F. Hale
Kathy Hayes
Helen Cozzens Healy

Betty Johnson
Zennetta Jones
Ivory Moore
Myrna Davis Nealey
Lorena E. Poppleton
Amy Sarah Pound, Assistant Director
Bettye J. Reed
Kent Rucker
Pearl J. Smith
Harold Thurman
Shireen I. Whitson
Lauren Wilhoite-Willis
Marianne E. Wright
Elaine Yarcho

OTHER PARTICIPANTS

Craig Bowman, Consultant and Presenter
Bataki Camberlin, Presenter
Movement Free Dance Co., Presenters
Andrew Cozzens, Editor
Jack Cozzens, Business Manager
Marilyn Dallet, Volunteer
Billie Arlene Grant, Journalist
Kandance James, Consultant
Wallace Yvonne McNair, Consultant and
　Presenter
Abayomi Meeks, Presenter
Marci Moore, Presenter
Bill Potts, Presenter
Rose Roy, Organizational Assistant
Shelby Shrigley, Editor
Erle Swanson, Volunteer
Sergei Thomas, Presenter
Christopher S. Tucker, Photographer

MENTORS*

Genesia E. Andrews
Shumara D. Andrews
Aspen Aletha Burkett
Channon Caston
Joshua J. Herald
Melissa Hicks
Rebecca K. Hill
Claire A. Imatani
Duane L. James
Michael Johnson
Dorothy Poppleton
Teisha Sheree Rollins
Nyeema A. Swanson
Akilah M. Thompson
Terrance Wright
Terrianne Wright

*High school students who assisted the
younger students in illustrating and writing
the book.

INDEX

The Quill Hedgehog Adventures Series

Green fiction for young readers. Each title is written by John Waddington-Feather and illustrated by Doreen Edmond.

Quill's Adventures in the Great Beyond
BOOK ONE
$5^1/2''$ x $8^1/2''$, 96 pages, $5.95, paper

Quill's Adventures in Wasteland
BOOK TWO
$5^1/2''$ x $8^1/2''$, 132 pages, $5.95, paper

Quill's Adventures in Grozzieland
BOOK THREE
$5^1/2''$ x $8^1/2''$, 132 pages, $5.95, paper

The Kidding Around Travel Guides

All of the titles listed below are 64 pages and $9.95 except for *Kidding Around the National Parks* and *Kidding Around Spain*, which are 108 pages and $12.95.

"A combination of practical information, vital statistics, and historical asides."

—New York Times

Kidding Around Atlanta
Kidding Around Boston, 2nd ed.
Kidding Around Chicago, 2nd ed.
Kidding Around the Hawaiian Islands,
Kidding Around London
Kidding Around Los Angeles
Kidding Around the National Parks of the Southwest
Kidding Around New York City, 2nd ed.
Kidding Around Paris
Kidding Around Philadelphia
Kidding Around San Diego
Kidding Around San Francisco

Kidding Around Santa Fe
Kidding Around Seattle
Kidding Around Spain
Kidding Around Washington, D.C., 2nd ed.

ORDERING INFORMATION
If you send us money for a book not yet available, we will hold your money until we can ship you the book. Your books will be sent to you via UPS (for U.S. destinations). UPS will not deliver to a P.O. Box; please give us a street address. Include $3.75 for the first item ordered and $.50 for each additional item to cover shipping and handling costs. For air-mail within the U.S., enclose $4.00. All foreign orders will be shipped surface rate; please enclose $3.00 for the first item and $1.00 for each additional item. Please inquire about foreign air-mail rates.

METHOD OF PAYMENT
Your order may be paid by check, money order, or credit card. We cannot be responsible for cash sent through the mail. All payments must be made in U.S. dollars drawn on a U.S. bank. Canadian postal money orders in U.S. dollars are acceptable. For VISA, MasterCard, or American Express orders, include your card number, expiration date, and your signature, or call (800) 888-7504. Books ordered on American Express cards can be shipped only to the billing address of the cardholder. Sorry, no C.O.D.'s. Residents of sunny New Mexico, add 6.125% tax to the total.

Address all orders and inquiries to:
John Muir Publications
P.O. Box 613
Santa Fe, NM 87504
(505) 982-4078
(800) 888-7504